First World War
and Army of Occupation
War Diary
France, Belgium and Germany

36 DIVISION
107 Infantry Brigade
Princess Victoria's (Royal Irish Fusiliers)
1st Battalion
1 August 1917 - 31 December 1917

WO95/2502/2

The Naval & Military Press Ltd
www.nmarchive.com
Published in association with The National Archives

Published by

The Naval & Military Press Ltd

Unit 10 Ridgewood Industrial Park,

Uckfield, East Sussex,

TN22 5QE England

Tel: +44 (0) 1825 749494

www.naval-military-press.com

www.nmarchive.com

This diary has been reprinted in facsimile from the original. Any imperfections are inevitably reproduced and the quality may fall short of modern type and cartographic standards.

© Crown Copyright
Images reproduced by permission of The National Archives, London, England, 2015.

Contents

Document type	Place/Title	Date From	Date To
Heading	WO95/2502/2		
Heading	1st Bn. Roy. IR. Fns 107 Bde 36 Div. France 1917 Aug-1917 Dec From 4 Div 10 Bde To 108 Bde 36 Div		
Miscellaneous	Preliminary Instruction No. 6	19/11/1917	19/11/1917
Heading	War Diary Of 1st Battalion Royal Irish Fusiliers. For Period 1-8-1917 To 31-8-1917 Vol 37		
War Diary	In The Field	01/08/1917	31/08/1917
Miscellaneous	1st Battn Royal Irish Fus. France	01/08/1917	01/08/1917
Miscellaneous	Two Collas Cad fes were also Seat to the Major at his request. He Proposed Attaching than to the cases with a Suitable insenption.		
Miscellaneous	1st R. Warwickshire R. 2nd Seaforth Highrs	01/08/1917	01/08/1917
Miscellaneous	Officer Commanding, 1st. Royal Irish Fusiliers	01/08/1917	01/08/1917
Miscellaneous	Operation Orders By Lieut. Colonel, A.B. Incledon-Webber, D.S.O. Commanding 1st Battn. Royal Irish Fusiliers "B"	05/08/1917	05/08/1917
Miscellaneous	Operation Order By Lieut. Colonel A.B. Incledon-Webber, D.S.O., Commanding 1st Battalion Royal Irish Fusiliers "C"	17/08/1918	17/08/1918
Miscellaneous	Operation Order By Lieut. Colonel A.B. Incledon-Webber, D.S.O., Commanding 1st Battalion Royal Irish Fusiliers "D"	22/08/1917	22/08/1917
Miscellaneous	1st Battn. Royal Irish Fusiliers "E"	31/08/1917	31/08/1917
Miscellaneous	Operation Order By Lieut. Colonel A.B. Incledon-Webber, D.S.O., Commanding 1st Battalion Royal Irish Fusiliers "F"	27/08/1917	27/08/1917
Miscellaneous	Index To Appendixes Of War Diary	31/08/1917	31/08/1917
Operation(al) Order(s)	107th Infantry Brigade Order No. 171 Appendix XXXV	26/08/1917	26/08/1917
Heading	War Diary Of 1st Battalion Royal Irish Fusiliers. Period 1-9-1917 To 30-9-17 Vol 38		
War Diary	In The Field	01/09/1917	26/09/1917
Miscellaneous	March Table To Accompany 107th Brigade Order No. 171		
War Diary	In The Field	27/09/1917	30/09/1917
Miscellaneous	Operation Orders By Lieut. Colonel A.B. Incledon-Webber, D.S.O., Commanding 1st Battn. Royal Irish Fusiliers	02/09/1917	02/09/1917
Miscellaneous	List Of Appendixes To War Diary	01/10/1917	01/10/1917
Miscellaneous	A	01/08/1917	01/08/1917
Miscellaneous	Operation Order By Lieut. Colonel A.B. Incledon-Webber, D.S.O., Commanding 1st Battn. Royal Irish Fusiliers	08/09/1917	08/09/1917
Miscellaneous	Operation Order By Lieut. Colonel, A.B. Incledon-Webber, D.S.O., Commanding 1st Battalion Royal Irish Fusiliers	14/09/1917	14/09/1917
Miscellaneous	Operation Orders By Lieut. Colonel A.B. Incledon-Webber, D.S.O., Commanding 1st Battalion Royal Irish Fusiliers	20/09/1917	20/09/1917

Miscellaneous	Operation Order By Major S. U. L. Clements., Commanding 1st Battalion Royal Irish Fusiliers	27/09/1917	27/09/1917
Heading	War Diary Of 1st Battalion Royal Irish Fusiliers. Period 1-10-1917 To 31-10-1917 Vol 39		
Miscellaneous	Index To War Diary Of 1st Battalion Royal Irish Fusiliers List Of Appendixes	01/11/1917	01/11/1917
War Diary	In The Field	01/10/1917	31/10/1917
Miscellaneous	Operation Orders By Major. S.U.L. Clements Commanding. 1st Battn. Royal Irish Fusiliers	03/10/1917	03/10/1917
Miscellaneous	Operations Order By Major, S.U.L. Clements Commanding 1st Battalion Royal Irish Fusiliers.	08/10/1917	08/10/1917
Miscellaneous	Operation Order By Major, S.U.L. Clements Commanding, 1st Battn. Royal Irish Fusiliers.	14/10/1917	14/10/1917
Miscellaneous	Operation Orders By Major S.U.L. Clements., Commanding 1st Battalion Royal Irish Fusiliers.	20/10/1917	20/10/1917
Miscellaneous	Operation Orders By Major, S.U.L. Clements Commanding, 1st Battn. Royal Irish Fusiliers	26/10/1917	26/10/1917
Heading	War Diary Of 1st. Battalion Royal Irish Fusiliers. From 1-11-1917 To 30-11-1917 Vol 40		
Miscellaneous	Preliminary Instruction No. 10	19/11/1917	19/11/1917
War Diary	In The Field	01/11/1917	30/11/1917
Miscellaneous	Battalion Orders By Lieut. Colonel S. U. L. Clements., Commanding 1st Battalion Royal Irish Fusiliers	01/11/1917	01/11/1917
Miscellaneous	Battalion Orders By Lieut. Colonel S. U. L. Clements., Commanding 1st Battalion Royal Irish Fusiliers	06/11/1917	06/11/1917
Miscellaneous	Battalion Orders By Lieut. Colonel S. U. L. Clements., Commanding 1st Battalion Royal Irish Fusiliers	12/11/1917	12/11/1917
Miscellaneous	Operation Orders By Lieut. Col. S.U.L. Clements., Commanding 1st Battalion Royal Irish Fusiliers	16/11/1917	16/11/1917
Miscellaneous	Battalion Orders By Lieut. Colonel S. U. L. Clements., Commanding 1st Battalion Royal Irish Fusiliers	18/11/1917	18/11/1917
Miscellaneous	Preliminary Instruction No. 2 Appendix "F"	13/11/1917	13/11/1917
Miscellaneous	List Of Appendixes	03/12/1917	03/12/1917
Miscellaneous	Preliminary Instructions No 4	15/11/1917	15/11/1917
Miscellaneous			
Miscellaneous	A Form Messages And Signals		
Miscellaneous	Formation Of A Battalion In The Attack		
Miscellaneous	Preliminary Instruction No. 5	16/11/1917	16/11/1917
Miscellaneous	Special Battalion Order		
Miscellaneous	Preliminary Instruction No. 3	13/11/1917	13/11/1917
Miscellaneous	Malplaquet House, Marlborough Lines, Aldershot Appendix "H"	20/10/1917	20/10/1917
Miscellaneous	Operation Orders By Lieut. Colonel, M. J. Furnell., Commanding 1st Battalion Royal Irish Fusiliers	28/11/1917	28/11/1917
Miscellaneous	War Diary		
Miscellaneous	107th Infantry Brigade Instructions For The Offensive. Communications In The Attack. Appendix 5	18/11/1917	18/11/1917
Miscellaneous	Preliminary Instructions No 9	10/11/1917	10/11/1917
Miscellaneous	Preliminary Instruction No. 7		
Miscellaneous	Preliminary Instruction No. 6	18/11/1917	18/11/1917
Miscellaneous	To All Ranks Of The 87th		
Operation(al) Order(s)	Operation Order No 87	01/08/1917	01/08/1917
Heading	War Diary Of 1st. Battalion Royal Irish Fusiliers Period 1-12-17 To 31-12-17 Vol 41		
War Diary	In The Field	13/12/1917	27/12/1917
War Diary	In The Field	01/12/1917	31/12/1917

Miscellaneous   Appendix "A" War Diary 1st Battalion The Royal Irish Fusiliers

MO95 / 3569 / 2

1st Bn. Roy. Ir. Fus.
107° Bde 36° Div.
France (Jan 1917 – Jan 1918)

1917 AUG – 1917 DEC

From 4 Div 10 Bde

To 108 Bde 36 Div

SECRET.   Copy No. 7

Preliminary Instruction No. 8.

1. Capture of BOURLON WOOD and Village.

It is the Corps Commander's intention to capture BOURLON WOOD and the Village on Zero Day if possible. In this event the 62nd Division will hold a line from the village to the HINDENBURG SUPPORT LINE at E.28. Central where their Left Flank will rest.

The 36th Division will be responsible for prolonging the line from this point to a point of junction with the 58th Division on their left.

If the 109th Brigade have reached their final objective, the line will run from E.28. Central - E.27 Central to the Barricade on the CAMBRAI -BAPAUME Road at K.1.b.76.10.

In this case the above line will probably be taken over by the 108th Brigade, leaving the 107th and 108th Brigades available for the next day's operations. These 2 Brigades will be moved to the HINDENBURG SUPPORT LINE in E.10 and E.16 and to HUGHES SWITCH in the afternoon of Zero Day.

If the 109th Brigade have not reached their final objective the 107th Brigade will join up from E.22 Central down the HINDENBURG SUPPORT LINE and thence across the canal at the point where the 109th Brigade has reached. The 108th Brigade will remain in the area mentioned in the preceding para.

2. Action if BOURLON WOOD is not captured.

If it is not possible to capture BOURLON WOOD on Z Day the Line held by the 62nd Division will probably run in front GRAINCOURT to the factory and thence along the trench in E.27 about 200 yards beyond the CAMBRAI-BAPAUME ROAD, or by the most suitable line to join up with the Right of the 109th Brigade at whatever point that Brigade may have reached.

In this case the 107th and 108th Brigades will move over to the HINDENBURG SUPPORT LINE between HUGHES SWITCH and GEORGES STREET and will occupy these trenches for the night, preparatory to continuing the attack the next day.

3. Zero Plus 1 Day.

The Operations to be undertaken by the Division will depend on Zero plus 1 Day will depend on which of the situations described above obtains at the end of operations on Zero Day.

The 107th and 108th Brigades will be prepared to carry out the attack described in para.2 of these instructions or possibly to take BOURLON WOOD and Village if these have not been taken on Zero Day.

4. Crossing of CANAL DU NORD.

If the attack progresses as anticipated the 107th and 108th Brigades will move by the HERMIES-GRAINCOURT ROAD, Crossing the canal by the Bridge to be erected at the Road Crossing (K.15.a.

If this is not possible a Bridge for Infantry and Pack Transport will be laid across the canal SOUTH of the SPOIL BANK (K.29.c.)

Field,
19-11-17
                                              Captain and Adjutant,
                                              1st Battalion Royal Irish Fusiliers.

ADDENDUM.
Battalion Intelligence Parties will carry tape with which they will be prepared to mark out their Battn. Assembly position when their Battns. cross the Canal.

Vol 37

CONFIDENTIAL

WAR DIARY.

of

1st BATTALION ROYAL IRISH FUSILIERS.

FOR PERIOD

1-8-1917 TO 31-8-1917.

[signature]
Lieut.Colonel,
Commanding 1st Battalion Royal Irish Fusiliers.

Field,
31-8-17.

WAR DIARY

OR

INTELLIGENCE SUMMARY.

(Erase heading not required.)

Army Form C. 2118.

Place	Date	Hour	Summary of Events and Information	Remarks and references to Appendices
In the Field	1-8-17		Orders received to entrain ARRAS on August 2nd. The Battn. was relieved by the 2nd Seaforth Highlanders and moved to Stirling Camp. 2 O/R Shell cases from POPUM presented to Mayor of ARRAS.	A.1.17. See Appendix
	2-8-17		The Divisional Commander saw the Battn. on parade at 9 a.m. and expressed his extreme regret that the Battn. was leaving the 4th Division in which it had served continuously throughout the campaign. The Battn. left camp for Railway Station ARRAS at 2-30 p.m. The Pipes of the 2nd Seaforth Highlanders accompanied the Battn. for about 1000 yards when the Drums of the Household Battn. met the Battn. and accompanied it until met by the drums of the 1st Royal Warwickshire Regt. who in turn were replaced by the 4th Divisional Band who played the Battn. into the Station. The following were at the Station to say goodbye to the Battn.:- Corps Commander- Sir C.Ferguson, Divisional Commander-Maj.Gen.Hon.W.Lambton, B.G.R.A.Div.Artillery-Br.Genl.Sykes, B.G.C.10th Bde.-Br.Genl.A.Pritchard, B.G.C.C.11th Bde.-Br.Genl.Berners, and various other officers of the Brigade and Division. The train left ARRAS at 4-54 p.m. Played out of the Station by the pipes of the 2nd Seaforth Highlanders who had followed the Battn. there for that purpose. From the commencement of the campaign the Battn. had been closely associated with the 2nd Battn. Seaforth Highlanders, having on almost occasions been next each other both in trenches and Action. This compliment was much appreciated. Captain G.W.T.BAREFOOT and 2/Lieut.W.D.BRADLEY rejoined the Battn. before entraining. The Battn. detrained at 4-0 a.m. at ABEELE and moved into camp at POPERINGHE H.S.a. coming under command of the 36th Division as Divisional troops. Heavy rain all day.	See Appendix "A"2.
	3-8-17		Captain J.W.O'DONOVAN resumed command of "C" Coy. and Captain BAREFOOT that of "D" Coy. The Battn. did not move. Rain.	
	4-8-17			
	5-8-17		Battn. did not move. Clearer weather.	
	6-8-17		Battn. moved at 7-30 a.m. and proceeded by route march to Billets (No.3 Area) South of WATOU. The Rev. J.H.McShane, M.C. returned to the 4th Division.	See Appendix "B".
	7-8-17		Training in No. 3. Area commenced.	

WAR DIARY
or
INTELLIGENCE SUMMARY.
(Erase heading not required.)

Army Form C. 2118.

Instructions regarding War Diaries and Intelligence Summaries are contained in F.S. Regs., Part II. and the Staff Manual respectively. Title pages will be prepared in manuscript.

Place	Date	Hour	Summary of Events and Information	Remarks and references to Appendices
	8-8-17		Training continued. Major P.E.Kelly was appointed Commandant Div. Troops and left the Battn. this day.	
	9-8-17		Training continued.	
	10-8-17		Training continued.	
	11-8-17		Training continued. 2/Lieut. E.H.McClenaghan to "C" Coy. 2/Lieut.J.McClure to "B" Coy. 2/Lieut. J.L.Driscoll to "B" Coy. joined this day and were posted to Coys. as shown.	
	12-8-17		Divine Service WATOU.	
	13-8-17		Training continued.	
	14-8-17		2/Lieut. H.S.Lee rejoined from T.M.B. and posted to "D" Coy. 2/Lieut. J.L.Chalmers rejoined from Musketry and reposted to "D" Coy.	
	15-8-17		Training continued. Voluntary service WATOU.	
	16-8-17		Training continued. Weather fine.	
	17-8-17		Training continued. Weather fine.	
	18-8-17		The Battn. moved to WINNEZEELE area and reached camp 4-30 p.m. Attached to 109th Inf.Bde.	See Appx.C.
	19-8-17		Battn. did not move.	
	20-8-17		Route march. Preliminary orders received for move on 23rd to BAPAUME area.	

Army Form C. 2118.

WAR DIARY
or
INTELLIGENCE SUMMARY.
(Erase heading not required.)

Instructions regarding War Diaries and Intelligence Summaries are contained in F. S. Regs., Part II. and the Staff Manual respectively. Title pages will be prepared in manuscript.

Place	Date	Hour	Summary of Events and Information	Remarks and references to Appendices
In the Field.	21-8-17		Battn. remained in camp at WINNEZEELE.	
	22-8-17		Battn. remained in camp at WINNEZEELE.	
	23-8-17		The Battn. entrained at CASTRE. Train leaving 11 p.m.	See Apdx. D.
	24-8-17		The Battn. detrained at BAPAUME 10 a.m. and moved by route march BARASTRE coming under orders of G.O.C. 107th Inf. Bde. on arrival. Strength of Battn. 29 Officers 692 Other Ranks.	
	25-8-17		The Battn. did not move. Front line north of METZ reconnoitred by officers.	
	26-8-17		The Battn. did not move. The aniversary of LE CATEAU was celebrated by the officers of the Battn. dining together. The Sergts. of the Battn. were entertained by the officers at a smoking concert. During the afternoon Officers and Men who had been with the Battn. at Le CATEAU in August, 1914 paraded and were congratulated by the C.O. 6 officers and 84 Other Ranks were on parade. 1 O.R. on duty 2 O.R. on leave. For nominal roll vide appendix.	See Apdx. E.
	27-8-17		The Battn. moved to NEUVILLE. Rain and heavy wind.	
	28-8-17		The Battn. moved to teres and Billets in METZ forming Bde. Reserve on arrival and relieving the 2nd Battn. South African Regt.	See Apdx. F.
	29-8-17		METZ systematically demolished. Clearing of debris and reroofing where possible commenced, to provide shelter accommodation.	
	30-8-17		The Battn. Found Working Parties 250 men for forward areas and trenches.	
	31-8-17		As for the 30th.	

[signature]
Lieut.-Colonel,
Commanding 1st Battalion Royal Irish Fusiliers.

Copy.

1st Batt. Royal Irish Lus.
France.
1. Aug. 1917.

To. Mons. Le Maire.
Arras.

I have two brass cartridge cases of a 24 c/m German gun, which was at one time in action at ROEUX and which was no doubt among others responsible for the damage done to your beautiful city —

The 1st Batt. Royal Irish Lusts (late 87th Foot) would esteem it a great honour if you would, on behalf of the Town of ARRAS accept these cartridge cases as souvenirs of the fighting April & May 1917 —

It might interest you to know that the most cherished badge of this Regt is the emblem of the eagle of France — won in remembrance of a great fight fought at BARROSA in 1811. —

Our pride in this badge has immeasurably increased, since we have had the honour on more than one occasion to fight shoulder to shoulder with your gallant troops —

A B Shakleton Webbe Lt Col.
Comdg 1st Bn R Irish Lus.

Two Collar badges were also sent to the Mayor at his request. He proposed attaching them to the cases with a suitable inscription.

Household Bn.
1st R. Warwickshire R.
2nd Seaforth Highrs.

   With reference to the departure of the 1st. Royal Irish Fusiliers from the BLUE LINE tomorrow.

   The Brigadier General accepts the offers of the Household Battalion, 1st R. Warwickshire Regt., and 2nd Seaforth Highrs., to lend their bands to play out the above mentioned Battalion.

   The O.C., 1st Royal Irish Fusiliers, would be glad if the band of the 2nd Seaforth Highlanders would place themselves at the head of the Battalion at the Road Junction H.13.b.5.5. at 2.20 p.m. tomorrow, they will play the Battalion as far as H.13.a.0.4. where they will fall out. The band of the Household Battalion will then take the place of the 2nd Seaforth Highlanders' band at H.13.a.0.4. and play as far as the Cross Roads, BLANGY, G.13.c.5.4. where it will fall out, their place then being taken by the band of the 1st. Royal Warwickshire Regt. who will play to the bend in the road at G.23.a.4.2. where they will fall out, their place being taken by the 4th Divisional band.

   The above mentioned bands should rendezvous as follows:-

2nd Seaforth Highrs.	Road Junction H.13.b.5.5.	2.20 p.m.
Household Bn.	H.13.a.0.4.	2.30 p.m.
1st R. Warwickshire R.	Branch Cross Roads G.13.c.5.4.	2.45 p.m.
Divisional Band.	Bend in the Road G.23.a.4.2.	2.55 p.m.

               Captain, S.C.
1/8/17.   10th Infantry Brigade.

<u>Copy to 4th Division.</u>

4 D.a
18/529

"A" 2

Officer Commanding,

    1st. Royal Irish Fusiliers

    I wish to express on behalf of the Officers, N.C.Os. and men of the 4th. Divisional Artillery our deep regret at the departure of the Royal Irish Fusiliers to another Division after having had the honour of serving with them so long.

    The Gunners feel they are losing a Battalion the covering of which has always been an easy and grateful task.

    We wish all ranks of the Battalion the best of luck and hope we may serve together again before long.

                                    Brigadier-general

1/8/17.   Commanding 4th. Divisional Artillery

"B"

Operation Orders
by
Lieut. Colonel, A.B. INCLEDON-WEBBER, D.S.O,
Commanding 1st Battn. Royal Irish Fusiliers.
5-8-1917.

1. **Move.** Reference Sheet 5 a (HAZEBROUCK).
The Battn. will move to WATOU (No. 3 Area) tomorrow.
Breakfasts will be at 6-15 a.m.
Parade at 7-0 a.m.
Right Markers to report to the R.S.M. at 6-55 a.m.
Order of march- Drums, Hd.Qrs.- D-A-B-C. Coy's, Transport.
200 yards between Coys and transport until the Battn.
is clear of POPERINGHE.
Route:- Along road to Forge in H.2. 1¾ miles S.E. of WATOU
WATOU.
All articles for transport will be ready by 6-30 a.m.

Advance Party.
Lieut. N.E.V.DICKS, with 3 H.Q.Signallers and 2 Orderlies
will parade with bicycles at 5 a.m. and will proceed and
report to the Area Commandant WATOU. An orderly will be
sent to the Inn on the POPERINGHE-Forge road (as mention-
-ed above) to meet the Battn. after location of Billets
has been ascertained.

(sd) W.SCOTT, Captain and Adjutant
1st Battn. Royal Irish Fusiliers.

"C"

Operation Oreder
by
Lieut.Colonel A.B.INGLEDON-WEBBER,D.S.O.,
Commanding 1st Battalion Royal Irish Fusiliers.
17-8-18.

1. MOVE.

The Battalion will move from this Area to WINNEZEELE Area tomorrow.
The Battalion will parade on the road outside HOWE CAMP at 2-0 p.m. with Head of Column facing WATOU.
Order of March :- Drums-Hd.Qrs.-A-B-C-D,Coys.-Transport.
All articles for transport will be ready by 1-45 p.m.

Advance Party consisting of Lieut.N.E.V.Dicks, 1 n.c.o. per Coy. and 2 Hd.Qrs. Orderlies, will parade with bicycles at 9-20 a.m. at the Orderly Room and will proceed to J.12.b.97. DROGLANT and report at 10 a.m. to staff officer 36th Division.

(sd) W.Scott, Captain and Adjutant
1st Battn. Royal Irish Fusiliers.

"D"

Operation Order
by
Lieut. Colonel A.B.INCLEDON-WEBBER, D.S.O.,
Commanding 1st Battalion Royal Irish Fusiliers.

22-8-17.

****

1. MOVE

The Battalion will entrain tomorrow at CASTRE.
Reference Sheet HAZEBROUCK 5 a (Square 3 H).
Route- WINNEZEELE-STEENVORDE-CASTRE.
"A" Coy. with one cooker and one G.S.Limber, 2 Pack horses and one officer's charger, will depart from CASTRE at 6-30 p.m. by train, they will parade in camp at 2-0p.m. and report to the R.T.O. at CASTRE at 5-0 p.m. they will proceed accompanied by the 150th Coy.R.E. and No.4 Train Coy. from CASTRE.
Transport for "A" Coy. will leave this Camp at 1-0 p.m.

Remainder of the Battn. will leave CASTRE Station by train at 10-30 p.m.

The Battn. less "A" Coy. will parade at 5-30 p.m.
Right Markers to report to the R.S.M. at 5-25 p.m.
Order of March- Drums- Hd.Qrs.- C-D-B.Coys. 300 yards distance between Coys.
Water bottles will be filled before marching off.
Transport will start from camp at 5 p.m. and arrive at CASTRE at 7-30 p.m. Articles for transport will be ready by 3-30 p.m.
The Battalion will entrain ½ hour before time of departure.
Train journey will last about 9 hours.
Caution.
All doors of covered trucks or carriages on the right hand side of the train when on the main line should be kept closed.

(sd) W.SCOTT, Captain and Adjutant
1st Battn.Royal Irish Fusiliers.

"E"

1st Battn. Royal Irish Fusiliers.

Nominal Roll of Officers, W.O's, N.C.O's and Men present with the Battn. on 26th August 1917, who participated in Battle of LE CATEAU, 26-8-14.

Regtl.No.	Rank	and Name.	Reg.No.	Rank	and Name.
	Lt.Col.	A.B.Incledon-Webber D.S.O.		Captain	M.J.W.O'Donovan,M.C.
	Captain	G.W.N.Barefoot,M.C.		Captain	H.A.MacMullen,M.C.
	Lieut.	G. Reeve,M.C.		2/Lieut.	S.G.Wolsey.
	Captain & Q.M.,	T.E.Bunting.	9571	R.Q.M.S.	H.Lyne.
8333	C.S.M.	R.Neville	10387	C.S.M.	H.Goode.
9368	C.Q.M.S.	F.Calloway	27510	Sergt.	D.W.J.Steele
9428	Sergt.	G.A.Williams	8375	"	S.Rosbotham
10985	"	C.Nicholson	11039	"	W.Speers
10514	"	J.Donnelly	6807	"	W.Clarke
10363	"	M.Moore	11015	"	J.Mitchell
10235	"	C.H.Steele	10452	"	O.Lloyd
10853	"	P.McGaley	10542	"	D.Barry
6092	"	J.Carey	9290	"	F.Smith
8630	"	B.Willis	10033	"	C.Austin
11153	"	T.Ashford	11193	"	T.Hutchinson
9062	"	E.Boyle	10356	"	A.Skingle
8740	"	C.Jones	10400	Corpl.	J.Boyd
8609	Corpl.	W.McCart	10183	"	C.Neville
9219	"	J.Kelly	11316	"	W.MaGill
10277	"	P.Grimes	10539	"	T.Ward
9810	"	C.Robinson	9722	"	J.Foley
9140	L.Cpl.	P.Vallely	8070	L.Cpl.	H.Wilson
7966	"	P.McManus	10171	"	W.Herbert
10652	"	F.Ryan	11221	"	J.Sweeney
8721	"	P.Brown	10328	"	J.Evans
7658	Pte.	J.Bicker	8872	Pte.	R.Bosworth
8761	"	M.Barker	11240	"	F.Barkley
8759	"	W.Colburn	11216	"	W.Gregg
9393	"	C.Hilliard	10407	"	G.Hadden
9437	"	J.Lewis	9680	"	P.McVeigh
11170	"	M.Murtagh	11318	"	R.McConville
11138	"	H.Rice	8892	"	J.Hanley
9221	"	J.Trainer		"	H.Graham
8411	"	O.Brady	7388	"	W.Marks
8344	"	J.Allen	8241	"	F.Evans
10448	"	T.Woods	8172	"	R.Black
8047	"	J.McClean	8085	"	P.Bannon
10359	"	E.McKendrick	7541	"	M.Lyster
10773	"	H.Adair	11385	"	T.Gibney
n9327	"	W.Hollis	8715	"	J.Joiner
9621	"	W.Porter	6682	"	W.Oxford
9336	"	F.Bailly	8971	"	J.Sharkey
10876	"	J.King	24590	"	T.Cullen
9217	"	M.Butler	8725	"	C.Bushel
8304	"	J.Conlon	7233	"	J.Dougan
8021	"	T.Davidson	9315	"	W.Jervis
11133	"	T.Leonard	19469	"	A.McKee
9291	"	H.Parker	24522	"	J.Reilly
9570	"	A.Walker	10333	"	G.Major
8402	"	S.Turkington	8362	"	W.Toland
8082	"	R.Plowman	9079	"	G.Ellis
10701	"	J.Donaldson	9951	"	M.McGrath
11186	"	E.Pearson	6945	"	D.Nelson
8093	"	A.Gordon	10942	"	D.O'Sullivan
10140	"	J.Cunniam	9732	"	R.Hagan
10357	"	W.Sullivan	22348	Corpl	C.Frost(Bedford Regt).

Field
31-8-17

Captain and Adjut.
1st Battn. Royal Irish Fusiliers.

"F"

Operation Order
by
Lieut.Colonel A.B.INCLEDON-WEBBER, D.S.O.,
Commanding 1st Battalion Royal Irish Fusiliers.
27-8-17.

1. <u>MOVE.</u>

    The Battn. will move tomorrow to Billets in METZ.
    The advance party proceeded today.
    The Battn. will parade on the road outside the Camp at 7-30 a.m.
    Order of March- Drums- Hd.Qrs.-A-B-C-D-Coys
    200 yards between coys. on marching off.
    All articles for transport will be ready by 7-0 a.m.
    The C.O. will inspect the Camp at 7-15 a.m.
    Breakfasts will be served on arrival of the Battn. at METZ.
    Guides will proceed with the cookers.
    Sick parade will be on arrival at METZ.

    (sd) W.SCOTT, Captain and Adjutant,
    1st Battn. Royal Irish Fusiliers.

INDEX to APPENDIXES of WAR DIARY.

No. of Index.	Purport.	Remarks.
A 1.	Copy of letter to the Mayor of ARRAS.	presenting Shell cases from ROEUX.
A 2.	Operation Order- move of Battn. from ARRAS to join 36th Division.	Letter from 10th Infantry Brigade detailing Bands etc to the Station. Letter from Br.Genl. C.A.SYKES Commanding 4th Division Artillery, expressing regret at the Battn. leaving 4th Div.
"B"	Operation Order for move of the Battn. from POPERINGHE to WATOU (No.3 Area).	
"C"	Operation Order for move of the Battn. from WATOU to WINNEZEELE Area.	
"D"	Operation Order for move of the Battn. from WINNEZEELE to BAPAUME Area.	
"E"	Nominal Roll of Officers, present with Battn. on 26th Aug.1917, who participated in Battle of LE CATEAU on August 26th 1914.	
"F"	Operation Order for move of the Battn. to METZ.	

Field
31-8-17

Lieut.Colonel,
Commanding 1st Battn. Royal Irish Fusiliers.

Appendix XXXI

SECRET   Copy No. 28

107th INFANTRY BRIGADE ORDER NO. 171.

Ref. Sheet 57c. 1/40,000.   26th August 1917.

1. The 107th Infantry Brigade will relieve the SOUTH AFRICAN Infantry Brigade in the TRESCAULT Sector on the 28th and 29th Insts. in accordance with the attached table.

2. (a) The extent of the Brigade front will be from Q.5.d.85.10 to Q.3.b.75.60.
   (b) The Division between the Right and Left Sub-sectors will be Q.5.c.20.87 - Q.4.d.90.40 - Q.10.b.75.80 - Q.10.a.90.50 - Q.9.d.40.00.

3. All details of relief will be arranged between Officers Commanding Units concerned.

4. The 10th and 15th R.I. Rifles will each send one Officer and 4 O.R's per Company to report to Battalion Headquarters Right and Left Sub-sectors respectively at 6 p.m. on the 27th Inst. These Officers and O.R's will remain in the line until the arrival of their Units.
   The South African Brigade are leaving an equivalent number behind for 24 hours after relief.

5. (a) All defence schemes, air photos, trench maps and programmes of work will be taken over.
   (b) All Camp equipment, etc. will be taken over and receipts given. A duplicate copy will be forwarded to Brigade Headquarters.

6. Advanced parties from the 1st R.I. Fusiliers and 8th/9th R.I. Rifles will report at 4.30 p.m. 27th Inst. as follows :-
        8th/9th R.I.R. to Major HUNT. V.10.a.7.9.
        1st R.I.Fus. to H.Q. 2nd Regiment in METZ.

7. (a) Units proceeding by rail will entrain at about P.26.c.90.20.
   (b) Each truck holds 25 O.R's.
   (c) The leading Company of each Unit will arrive 30 minutes before scheduled time for entraining to commence.

8. Units moving by road will maintain 200 yards interval between Companies.

9. All Quartermasters and Transport Officers must make themselves acquainted with the system of supply by road and railway.

10. Completion of reliefs will be reported to Brigade Headquarters by the code word "PAST".

                                              P. T. O.

11. G.O.C. 107th Brigade will assume command of the TRESCAULT Sector on completion of Infantry reliefs on the 28th Inst., and Brigade Headquarters will open at METZ, Q.20.c.7.8, at 6 p.m.

ACKNOWLEDGE.

T.O.M. Buchan
Captain.
Brigade Major.
107th Infantry Brigade.

Issued at 11 p.m.

Issued to :-

Copy No. 1 to 1st R.I. Fus.
" " 2 to 8th R.I.R.
" " 3 to 9th R.I.R.
" " 4 to 10th R.I.R.
" " 5 to 15th R.I.R.
" " 6 to 107 M.G. Coy.
" " 7 to 107 T.M. Bty.
" " 8 to 9th Div "G"
" " 9 to 9th Div "Q"
" " 10 to 36th Div "G"
" " 11 to 36th Div "Q"
" " C.R.A. 9th Div.
" " C.R.E.
" " 14 to A.D.M.S.
" " 15 to A.P.M.
" " 16 to D.A.D.O.S.
" " 17 to 108th Brigade.
" " 18 to 109th Brigade.
" " 19 to S.A. Brigade.
" " 20 to 9th Light Rly. Coy.
" " 21 to 121 Field Coy. R.E.
" " 22 to No. 2 Coy. Div. Train.
" " 23 to Town Major, YTRES.
" " 24 to Bde Signal Officer.
" " 25 to Bde Intelligence Officer.
" " 26 to Bde Transport Officer
" " 27 to War Diary.
" " 28 to War Diary ✓
" " 29 to File.

C O N F I D E N T I A L

W A R   D I A R Y.

of

1st BATTALION ROYAL IRISH FUSILIERS.

PERIOD:

1-9-1917   to   30-9-17.

[signature]

Major, for Lieut.Colonel,
Commanding 1st Battalion Royal Irish Fusiliers.

In the Field,
1-10-1917

WAR DIARY
or
INTELLIGENCE SUMMARY
(Erase heading not required.)

Army Form C. 2118.

Place	Date	Hour	Summary of Events and Information	Remarks and references to Appendices
In the Field.	1-9-17		2 Coys. Training and 2 Coys on Working Parties.	nil
	2-9-17		2 Coys. Training and 2 Coys on Working Parties.	nil
	3-9-17		The Battn. occupied Front line Trenches South of HAVRINCOURT relieving elements of the 10th Battn. Royal Irish rifles and the 11th Battn. Royal Irish Rifles. A.B.C.Coys in Front Line. D.Coy in support. Relief completed by 11-35 p.m. Quiet - Fine.	See Appendix "A" nil
	4-9-17		Exceptionally quiet. Trenches in fair condition. No revetment. Enemy activity restricted to consolidation of his position in depth - Patrol encounters with enemy covering parties- Fine.	nil
	5-9-17		Quiet- Improvement of wire and trenches continued- patrols as for 4th - Fine.	nil
	6-9-17		Quiet- As for 5th- Showery.	nil
	7-9-17		Quiet- A few shells into TRESCAULT. Fine.	nil
	8-9-17		Quiet- Patrol encounters but no identification obtained- Fine.	nil
	9-9-17		Quiet- The Battn. was relieved by the 10th Battn. Royal Irish Rifles and proceeded to camp at EQUANCOURT by light railway. Relief complete 11-35 p.m.	See Appendix "B". nil
	10-9-17		Inspection parades and cleaning up.	nil
	11-9-17		Such training as possible- 2½ Coys on working parties. Construction of Bayonet Fighting Course and Rifle Range commenced.	nil
	12-9-17		As for 11th.- At 2-45 a.m. the Corps Commander,Lieut.General Sir C.L.Woolcombe, K.C.B. inspected the Battn. on parade and also the Transport. At the conclusion of the inspection he complimented the Commanding officer on the turn out and appearance of the Battalion and the Transport. He desired that his appreciation should be conveyed to all concerned.	nil
	13-9-17		As for the 11th.	nil

Army Form C. 2118.

WAR DIARY
or
INTELLIGENCE SUMMARY

(Erase heading not required.)

Instructions regarding War Diaries and Intelligence Summaries are contained in F. S. Regs., Part II. and the Staff Manual respectively. Title Pages will be prepared in manuscript.

Place	Date	Hour	Summary of Events and Information	Remarks and references to Appendices
In the Field.	14-9-17		As for the 11th.	
	15-9-17		The Battalion relieved the 10th Battalion Royal Irish Rifles in the Trenches immediately WEST of TRESCAULT by light railway to TRESCAULT. Relief completed by 11-30 p.m.:- C.Coy.Left Coy.- B.Coy Centre Coy.- D.Coy.Right Coy.- A.Coy. in support. - Fine.	See Appendix "C" nil
	16-9-17		Quiet - Work on trenches and wiring continued - No enemy patrols encountered outside their wire. Enemy active in trench digging and wiring.	nil
	17-9-17		As for 16th.	nil
	18-9-17		As for 16th.- Slight increase in enemy artillery.- C.Coy lines and D.Coy lines shelled (about 20 rounds).- Fine.	nil
	19-9-17		As for 16th.- D.Coy lines and Sap registered.- Fine.	nil
	20-9-17		As for 16th.- D.Coy.lines shelled with 77m/m at 11 a.m. to 12 noon - registration.- Fine.	nil
	21-9-17		Intermittent shelling - The Battn. was relieved by the 10th Battn.Royal Irish Rifles and moved on relief to METZ. relief complete 9-30 p.m.	See Appendix "D" None
	22-9-17		Inspection parades and cleaning up.- Lieut.Colonel A.E.Incledon-Webber,D.S.O. proceeded on leave. Command of the Battn. taken over by Major S.U.L.Clements.- Weather fine - 3 Officers and 185 Other ranks found for working parties.	nil
	23-9-17		5 Officers and 345 Other ranks found for working parties - METZ shelled by 5.9's (about 50 shells) Weather fine.	nil
	24-9-17		5 Officers and 345 Other ranks found for working parties.- Weather fine.	nil
	25-9-17		As for 24th.	nil
	26-9-17		As for 24th.	nil

MARCH TABLE TO ACCOMPANY 107th BRIGADE ORDER NO. 171.

DATE	UNIT	MOVES TO	RELIEVING	ROUTE	REMARKS
AUG. 28th	15th R.I.R.	Right Sub-Sector.	3rd Regiment	By rail leaving P.26.c.80.20 at 10 a.m. Detrain Q.9.c. 11 a.m. where guides will meet.	30 minutes interval will be kept between Coys. from Q.9.c. onwards.
-do-	10th R.I.R.	Left Sub-Sector.	4th Regiment	By rail leaving P.26.c.80.20 at 8 p.m. Detrain Q.10.a.00.00 where guides will meet.	
-do-	1st R.I.F.	METZ (Brigade Reserve)	2nd Regiment	By Road. Head of column to arrive in METZ by 8:30 a.m.	Transport not to enter EQUANCOURT before 9 a.m.
-do-	8/9th R.I.R.	EQUANCOURT (Div. Reserve)	Details of S.A. Brigade	By road via road through P.34. and W.4. Head of column to enter EQUANCOURT at 8:30 a.m.	
29th	107 M.G.Coy.	Line. H.Q. METZ.	8 guns 28 M.G. Coy. Road Coy. 4 guns 197 R. M.G.Coy. H.Q. 28 M.G.Coy.		Details to be arranged between Os.C. Units concerned
-do-	107 T.M.Bty.	Line. H.Q. METZ.	S.A. Brigade T.M. Bty.	Road.	Guns will be taken over in the line, and guns handed over in their place.

Army Form C. 2118.

WAR DIARY
or
INTELLIGENCE SUMMARY
(Erase heading not required.)

Place	Date	Hour	Summary of Events and Information	Remarks and references to Appendices
In the Field:	27-9-17		Weather fine.- METZ shelled with 5.9's from 9-30 a.m. to 12 noon and from 7 p.m. to 7am. Casualties 3 Killed, 7 wounded. The Battn. relieved the 10th Royal Irish Rifles in same line as on Sept.15th.- Relief complete 9-45 p.m.- Captain J.W.O'Donovan,M.C., left to take over command of 56th Div.Depot Battn. A/Captain C.Drew took over command of "C" Coy.	See Appendix "B" enc.
	28-9-17		Weather fine - Usual work on trenches.	enc.
	29-9-17		Same as 28th.	enc.
	30-9-17		Same as 30th.	enc.
In the Field, 1-10-1917.				

OutClements
Major,
Commanding 1st Battalion Royal Irish Fusiliers.

"A"

Operation Orders
by
Lieut.Colonel A.B.INCLEDON-WEBBER,D.S.O.,
Commanding 1st Battn. Royal Irish Fusiliers.
In the Field, 2-9-17.

---

1. Move.

The Battalion will relieve the 10th Royal Irish Rifles from "C" Sap inclusive up to the Left of the present Sub-Sector and will also relieve the 13th Royal Irish Rifles (108th Bde.) up to OXFORD ROAD exclusive.
The Boundary now between Right and Left Sub-Sectors is "C" Sap inclusive to Left Sub-Sector--thence straight line to Q.9.d.5.2.
Dispositions of Coys. as in instructions already issued.
"A" Coy. will be Right Coy.   "B" Coy. will be centre Coy.
"C" "   "   " Left   "   "D" "   "   " Reserve "

Order of March to the trenches - Bn.Hd.Qrs.,B,C,A,D Coys.
Leading Coy. will move at 8-15 p.m. 100 yards between platoons.
10 minutes between Coys.
1 Limber will report to each Coy. and Battn. Hd.Qrs. at 7-15 p.m.
All maps and Trench Stores etc. will be taken over and Lists sent to Battn. Hd.Qrs. by 10 a.m. 4th Inst.
Coys will report relief complete by BAB Code and Orderly.

Guides and Advance Party.
1 Officer and 3 n.c.o's per Coy. will proceed to the line and take over during the morning and the N.C.O's will act as guides for each platoon under Coy. arrangements.

Routine.
Lists of Stores,Tents and Huts etc. to be handed over will be sent to the Orderly Room by 12 noon tomorrow.
"D" Coy. will detail 1 n.c.o. and 10 Men to stay behind and report to the Transport Officer for work on the Transport Lines.
The Orderly Room,Drums,and 1 Pioneers will remain with Major, S.U.L.CLEMENTS, at Old Battn. Hd.Qrs. while the Battn. is in the Line.

PACKS.
Packs will be taken into the Line.

(sd) W.SCOTT,Captain and Adjutant,
1st Battalion Royal Irish Fusiliers.

List of Appendixes to War Diary.

Initial letter of Appendix.	Purport.	Remarks.
"A"	Operation Order dated 3-9-17 re. Battn. relieves 10th R.Ir.Rifles in the line.	
"B"	Operation Order dated 8-9-17 re. Relief of the Battn. by 10th R.Ir.Rifles.	
"C"	Operation Order dated 14-9-17 re. Battn. relieves 10th R.Ir.Rifles in the line.	
"D"	Operation Order dated 20-9-17 re. Battn. relieved by 10th R.Ir.Rifles.	
"E"	Operation Order dated 27-9-17 re. Battn. relieves 10th R.Ir.Rifles in the line.	

In the Field,
1-10-1917.

Ath Clements
Major,
Commanding 1st Battalion Royal Irish Fusiliers.

"A"

Transport 3 — Transport will arrive at Arras station at 1.50pm (water carts full)

Rations 4 — Rations for 3rd inst will be carried by battn 4th inst — on train in bulk

Articles for transport 5 — All articles for transport will be ready by 12.30pm except mess stuff. Mess stuff 1.30pm. Transport will arrive about 12.15pm

Dinners 6 — 12 noon.

Detraining Party 7 — 1 officer + 50 OR B Coy will be ready at detraining point for unloading

1.8.17.

"B"

Operation Order
by
Lieut.Colonel A.B.INGLEDOW-WEBBER,D.S.O.,
Commanding 1st Battn. Royal Irish Fusiliers.   In the Field, 2-9-17.

Relief.

1. The Battn. will be relieved by the 10th Royal Irish Rifles tomorrow night. On relief, the Battn. will proceed by trains to HOUANCOURT from TRESCAULT Railhead.

2. Lewis Guns, Mess kit etc. will go back by train.

3. Coys. will report relief complete by orderly.

4. Lists of stores to be handed over will be sent to Battn. Hd.Qrs. by 11 a.m.

5. Guides. 1 guide per platoon and 2 from Battn. Hd.Qrs. will report to Lieut.R.J.Willinson at "D" Coy.Hd.Qrs. at 8-0 p.m. to meet trains at Railhead.

6. Reports showing "Work Done" will be forwarded to Bn.Hd.Qrs. by 11 a.m.

(sd)W.SCOTT,Capt.& Adjt.
1st Battn. Royal Irish Fusiliers.

"C"

Operation Order
by
Lieut.Colonel,A.B.Incledon-Webber,D.S.O.,
Commanding 1st Battalion Royal Irish Fusiliers.,
In the Field,14-9-17.

1. Relief.

The Battn. will relieve the 10th Battn. Royal Irish Rifles in the line tonight. Disposition of the Battn. in the Line will be as follows:- D.Coy RIGHT Coy.- B.Coy.Centre Coy.- C.Coy.Left Coy.- A.Coy Reserve Coy.

Advance Party. 1 Officer and 2 N.C.O's per Coy will parade at 2-15 p.m. and will proceed to the trenches and take over stires etc. Coys. will make their own arrangements with Coys of the Royal Irish Rifles re. guides if any are required.

The Battn. will parade in camp at 6-30 p.m. and will march to entrain at P.29.c. at 7-15 p.m. for TRESCAULT. Order of March :- Hd.Qrs.-C.B.D.A.Coy. 1 marker per Coy will report to the R.S.M. on the parade ground at 6-45 p.m.

Lists of Trench Stores taken over will be sent to Battn. Hd.Qrs. by 11 a.m. on the 18th inst.

Returns to be rendered while in the trenches will be the same as for last tour:- Situation Reports at 3 a.m. and 3 p.m. Intelligence and Casualty Reports at 9-15 a.m. Copies of the Intelligence summary forms and patrol reports are issued to all concerned with Battn. Orders.

Relief Complete will be reported by Orderly.

All details other than the Regtl.Transport and the Qr.Mr. Staff will parade with the Battn. and will march to METZ under 2/Lieut. T.Houston M.C. This party will be billetted in METZ and will repo report to Major S.U.I.Clements at 8-30 p.m..

(sd) W.Scott, Captain and Adjutant,
1st Battalion Royal Irish Fusiliers.

"D"

Operation Orders
by
Lieut.Colonel A.B.INGLEDON-WEBBER, D.S.O.,
Commanding 1st Battalion Royal Irish Fusiliers.
In the Field, 20-9-17

-*-

1. <u>Relief.</u>
The Battn. will be relieved by the 10th Royal Irish Rifles tomorrow night and on relief will proceed to METZ, Coys taking over the same areas as last tour in METZ.
The 10th Royal Irish Rifles leave METZ at about 7-0 p.m.
Coys will report relief complete by orderly.
Lists of stores to be handed over and "Work Done" reports to be handed in at Battn. Hd.Qrs. by 9-15 a.m.
Lists of stores taken over in METZ will be handed in at Bn.Hd.Qrs. by 12 noon on the 22nd inst.
<u>Advance Party.</u>
1 Officer and 1 N.C.O from each Coy. and Battn. Hd.Qrs. will report during the day at METZ and take over.
Work being carried on by the 10th Royal Irish Rifles will be taken over.
<u>Water tins.</u>
"B" Coy will bring out 17 water tins and "C" Coy. 25 water tins and on arrival at METZ will hand them over to the detachment of R.A.M.C. attached to this Battn.
<u>Ammunition.</u>
All N.C.O's and Men will be made up with the correct amount of S.A.A. before leaving the line. A report will be furnished by 9-0 a.m. on the 25th inst to the effect that all ranks are complete in S.A.A. according to War Establishment.
<u>Transport.</u>
1 Limber each will be at TRESCAULT Railhead at 9-15 p.m. for "A" and "D" Coys.
1 Limber each for Bn.Hd.Qrs., "B" and "C" Coys. will be at Battn. Hd.Qrs. at 9-45 p.m.

2. <u>Courts Martial.</u>
A F.G.C.M. will assemble at 108th Field Ambulance at 10 a.m. tomorrow for the trial of the undermentioned. All witnesses will parade at 9-0 a.m. and will report to 2/Lieut.G.REEVE,M.C. at 108th Field Ambulance, ROYAULCOURT, at 10 a.m.
No.8104 Pte. W.CLARKE, "A" Coy.
No.23676 "   T.COCHRANE "D" Coy.

****

<u>ROUTINE, WORK, etc., for 22-9-1917.</u>

1. <u>Duties Officers.</u>
Battn. Orderly Officer :-   2/Lieut.R.C.EATON.

2. <u>Duty Company.</u>
Duty Coy. :-   "B" Company.

3. <u>Roll Call.</u>
C.O's Roll Call at :-   9-30 a.m.

4. <u>Office.</u>
C.O's Office will be at :-   2-0 p.m.

5. <u>Sick.</u>
Sick Parade will be at :-   10-0 a.m.

6. <u>Returns.</u>
Coys will render to Orderly Room by 10-30 a.m. a return showing numbers in Coys. available for work and how remainder are employed.

P.T.O.

7. **Working Parties etc.**

   The Duty Coy. will furnish the following parties daily :-
   (a) 1 N.C.O. and 10 Men to report to the Town Major, METZ at 8-30 a.m. and 2-30 p.m. for general work in METZ.

   (b) 1 N.C.O. and 3 Men, Gas and Aeroplane Guard at the Bde. Baths mounting with Battn. Duties.

   (c) 1 N.C.O. and 10 Men for work under Sergt. Moore, reporting at 9-0 a.m. daily.

   Party (b) will go down to take over at 4 p.m. tomorrow and will report at R.I.F. Orderly Room at METZ for instructions ref. guard. Sentry to be provided with a whistle.

                              Captain and Adjutant,
                              1st Battn. Royal Irish Fusiliers.

Operation Order
by
Major S. U. L. CLEMENTS.,
Commanding 1st Battalion Royal Irish Fusiliers.,
In the Field, 27-9-17.

1. Relief.

The Battn. will relieve the 10th Royal Irish Rifles in the line tomorrow
Disposition of the Battn. in the Line will be as follows :-
D.Coy. Right Coy, A.Coy. Centre Coy. C.Coy Left Coy B.Coy Reserve.
Advance Party:. 1 Officer and 2 N.C.O's per Coy will parade at the
Orderly Room at 2-15 p.m. and proceed to the trenches to take over
stores etc. and will make arrangements re. guides if required.
Order of march to the Trenches :- Hd.Qrs. C.D.A.B.Coys. Leading
Coy will move at 7-0 p.m. 10 minutes between Coys. 100 yards
between platoons.
Transport:- 1 Limber will report to Battn. Hd.Qrs. and to each Coy
at 3-30 p.m. also 1 Limber will report at above hour for A and C
Cooks and 1 Limber for B and D Cooks.
All maps trench stores etc. will be taken over and a list sent to
Battn. Hd.Qrs. by 10-0a.m. 28th inst.
Coys. will report relief complete by orderly.
Lists of stores, Tents, huts etc. to be handed over will be sent to
the Orderly Room by 12 noon tomorrow.
The Orderly Room, Drums and 2 pioneers will remain with 2/Lieut T.
Houston, M.C. at Old Battn. Hd.Qrs.
Packs. Coys not wishing to take packs into the line will have them
stored in METZ under Coy. arrangements.

(sd) W.Scott, Captain and Adjutant,
1st Battalion Royal Irish Fusiliers.

Confidential.

WAR DIARY

of

1st BATTALION ROYAL IRISH FUSILIERS.

Period

1 - 10 - 1917   to   31 - 10 - 1917.

Ant Clemente
Lieut.Colonel,
Commanding 1st Battalion Royal Irish Fusiliers.

Field,
1-11-17

Index to War Diary of 1st Battalion Royal Irish Fusiliers
List of Appendixes.

No. of Appendix.	Purport.	Remarks.
"A"	Operation Order.	Relief of the Battn. by the 10th R.Ir.Rifles.
"B"	Operation Order.	Battalion Relieve the 10th Battn. R.Ir.Rifles.
"C"	Operation Order.	Relief of the Battn. by 10th R.Ir.Rifles.
"D"	Operation Order.	Battalion relieve the 10th R.Ir.Rifles.
"E"	Operation Order.	Relief of the Battn. by the 10th R.Ir.Rifles.

Field,
1-11-17.

AL Curvis
Lieut.Colonel,
Commanding 1st Battalion Royal Irish Fusiliers.

Army Form C. 2118.

WAR DIARY
or
INTELLIGENCE SUMMARY.
(Erase heading not required.)

Instructions regarding War Diaries and Intelligence Summaries are contained in F. S. Regs., Part II. and the Staff Manual respectively. Title pages will be prepared in manuscript.

Place	Date	Hour	Summary of Events and Information	Remarks and references to Appendices
In the Field.	1-10-17.		Weather fine. Work on trenches. Quiet. Brig.Gen.R.J.Kentish,D.S.O. on tour in France between courses of his Senior Officers School at Aldershot, visited the Battn. arriving at 8-0 p.m. Had dinner at Bn.Hd.Qrs. and went round the line about 10-30 p.m. Slept the night at Bn.Hd.Qrs.	nil
	2-10-17.		Weather fine. Work on Trenches. Casualties 2 Men and 2 wounded. Brig.Gen.Kentish went round line at 5-30 a.m. and before leaving complimented the Battn. by saying that, "Since he came to France in 1914 he never saw the Battn. in such a fine state of efficiency". He left after breakfast about 9-0 a.m. to visit 9th Bn.Roy.Irish Fusiliers. He brought with him on Oct.1st AMIENS pies, case of champagne for the officers, whiskey, cigarettes and papers for the N.C.O's, and cigarettes and papers for the men.	nil
	3-10-17		Weather fine. Quiet. Battn. were relieved by the 10th R.Ir.Rifles, and on relief about 9-30 p.m. proceeded by train from TRESCAULT to EQUANCOURT becoming Divisional Reserve. Temp.Capt.W.H. Crotty rejoined from Senior Officers School,Aldershot.	See Appx. "A" nil
	4-10-17.		Weather wet, cold and stormy. Cleaning up and taking of deficiencies. Burial Service held at METZ for other ranks killed at end of tour in the trenches. Preparation for sports with 9th Battn. Wire received that Lieut.Colonel A.B.Incleton-Webber,D.S.O. would proceed to take over command of 27th Infantry Brigade,12th Division.	nil
	5-10-17.		Battn. paraded at 8-40 a.m. and marches to RUYAULCOURT for sports in conjunction with 9th Bn. Royal Irish Fusiliers. Day was showery but did not interfere with sports. Events were very evenly contested and a very enjoyable day was spent. Massed drums of 1st and 9th Battn. and Divisional Band played selections throughout the day. 24th M.A.C. Concert Party "The Wayfarers" gave a concert in the evening. Some of the officers and sergeants remained for dinner. Battn. returned to EQUANCOURT Camp at 10-0 p.m.	nil
	6-10-17.		Very wet. Training hindered. Lectures. Drainage of Camp and making of fireplaces.	nil
	7-10-17		Lieut.Colonel A.B.Incleton-Webber returned from leave. Weather wet.	nil

Army Form C. 2118.

WAR DIARY
or
INTELLIGENCE SUMMARY.
(Erase heading not required.)

Instructions regarding War Diaries and Intelligence Summaries are contained in F. S. Regs., Part II. and the Staff Manual respectively. Title pages will be prepared in manuscript.

Place	Date	Hour	Summary of Events and Information	Remarks and references to Appendices
In the Field.	8-10-17.		Training continued. Weather fine but windy. Lieut.Col.A.B.Incledon-Webber,D.S.O., addressed the Battn. on parade in following terms " Fusiliers- I have been appointed to command the 27th Infantry Brigade and leave here this afternoon - I came out with the Battn. in 1914 and with the exception of about 15 months have been with it ever since. As far as war can be made pleasant the pleasantest times that I have spent during the campaign have been with the Battn.- The loyalty, endurance and behaviour of all ranks both in action and billets has made my period of command a very pleasant and assured one, and I shall always regard with pride the fact that I have had the honour to command so fine a Battn.- in spite of all we have gone through since 1914 the best traditions of the regiment are maintained as I trust they always will be. I wish all ranks the best of luck and all the success they deserve and I look forward to the time when this grim business being brought to a satisfactory issue I may be permitted to return." Major S.U.L.CLEMENTS then called for 3 cheers for Brig.Genl.Incledon-Webber- which was heartily responded to. Brig.Genl.Incledon-Webber, "I may be a Brigadier but an Irish Fusilier always".	
	9-10-17.		Very wet. Battn.relieved the 10th R.Ir.Rifles, in same line as Sept.27th. Relief was complete by 10-0 p.m. Capt.H.A.MacMullen,M.C. returned from Lewis Gun Course and took over command of "A" Coy. Captain C.Drew returned to "B" Coy. 1 Man "D" Coy wounded by shell. Trenches very wet and dirty.	See Appx. "B".
	10-10-17.		Weather wet. Usual trench work and routine in trenches. Special issue of rum to Battn. 2/Lieut.M.J.Parkhill joined the Battn. from Reinforcement.	
	11-10-17.		Very quiet. Weather fine. Usual trench routine.	
	12-10-17.		Very wet. Rum ration commenced. Quiet. Usual routine.	
	13-10-17.		Very quiet. Weather fine. Usual trench routine.	
	14-10-17.		Weather fine. Lieut.H.J.Fyans rejoined Battn. from No.1 Training Camp, ETAPLES.	See "Appx
	15-10-17.		Weather fine. Battn. relieved by 10th R.Ir.Rifles. Relief complete by 8-30 p.m.	
	16-10-17.		Weather fine. Cleaning up of billets in METZ. Captain.G.W.M.Barefoot,M.C. proceeded to join 9th Battn. as Adjutant.	

Army Form C. 2118.

WAR DIARY
or
INTELLIGENCE SUMMARY.
(Erase heading not required.)

Instructions regarding War Diaries and Intelligence Summaries are contained in F. S. Regs., Part II. and the Staff Manual respectively. Title pages will be prepared in manuscript.

Place	Date	Hour	Summary of Events and Information	Remarks and references to Appendices
In the Field	17-10-17.		Battn. working half by day and half by night.	ante
	18-10-17.		-do-	ante
	19-10-17.		-do-	ante
	20-10-17.		-do-	ante
	21-10-17.		The Battn. relieved the 10th R.Ir.Rifles in front line. Relief complete 7-45 p.m. Weather fine.	See APPX. "D". ante
	22-10-17.		Weather fine. Usual trench routine. Situation normal.	ante
	23-10-17.		Very quiet. Very wet.	ante
	24-10-17.		Weather fine. 2/Lieut.G.C.Watson while on patrol captured 1 wounded prisoner of 84th I.R. This patrol consisting of 2 officers and 14 other ranks went out and occupied an enemy post at dusk and were waiting for enemy to come in. One man, the prisoner, came forward to reconnoitre, he became suspicious and had to be shot while about 40 yards from the post. Remainder of enemy did not come on. 2/Lieut. WATSON with 2 other ranks went out and brought prisoner in.	ante
	25-10-17.		Weather fine but cold. Work in trenches and patrols as usual. 3 O.R's missing from one of our patrols. The patrol 1 officer and 10 other ranks attacked German post of 30 other ranks and inflicted casualties. On coming back 3 O.R's lost their way and must have been captured. Patrols were out and searched ground for them for over 12 hours after but no trace of missing men was found. One patrol under 2/Lieut.Watson gained a lot of useful information.	ante
	26-10-17.		Weather wet and blowy. Nothing unusual.	ante
	27-10-17.		Battn. relieved by 10th R.Ir.Rifles and on relief went to camp at EQUANCOURT, and became Divisional Reserve. Capt.W.A.FOLEY wounded by bullet at about 2,200 yards range. Wound serious.	See Appx. "E" ante
	28-10-17.		Weather fine. Cleaning up and taking of deficiencies, after tour in line..1st Match of Brigade Football league played against 8/9th R.Ir.Rifles. Battn. lost by 1 goal to Nil.	ante
	29-10-17.		Training. Weather fine.	ante

Army Form C. 2118.

WAR DIARY
or
INTELLIGENCE SUMMARY.
(*Erase heading not required.*)

Instructions regarding War Diaries and Intelligence
Summaries are contained in F. S. Regs., Part II.
and the Staff Manual respectively. Title pages
will be prepared in manuscript.

Place	Date	Hour	Summary of Events and Information	Remarks and references to Appendices
In the Field.	30-10-17.		Weather showery. Training continued. 2nd match of Brigade football league played against 107th Machine Gun Coy. Resulted in a win for the Battn. by 4 goals to 1. Warning Order received for the Battn. to move to neighbourhood of YPRES.	one
	31-10-17.		The Battn. moved at 1-30 p.m. from EQUANCOURT to VAULULART Camp in P.28.d. ref.Sheet 57.c. and arrived 3-0 p.m. Weather fine.	one
Field, 1-11-17				

A. L. Clunie
Lieut.Colonel,
Commanding 1st Battalion Royal Irish Fusiliers.

Operation Orders
by
Major. S.U.J. Clements
Commanding, 1st Battn. Royal Irish Fusiliers

----

(1) Relief.   The Battalion will be relieved by the 10th R.I.R. and on relief will march to TRESCAULT railhead to entrain for EQUANCOURT.
2/Lt. E.J. PARKHILL will act as entraining officer.

Companies will report "Relief Complete" by orderly.

(2) Stores.   List of trench stores to be handed over to be sent to Battn. Hdqrs. by 9 am. to-morrow.
Great care to be taken that lists of stores are accurate as many errors have been made during last two tours.
Work completed and work in hand report to reach Bn. Hdqrs. by 11 am. to-morrow.

(3) Adv. Party.   1 N.C.O. per Company will parade at PLACE MONTEVERT at 2 pm. and proceed and report to Capt. W. Scott., M.C at EQUANCOURT at 3.30 pm.

(3) Deatched Parties.   Bde. Works party, Trench Wardens, and Cable party will rejoin Companies to-morrow evening at EQUANCOURT and will remain with Companies during tour in billets at that place.

(5) Lewis Guns.   All Lewis Guns will be taken in train. Limbers will meet train at G.M. Stores to carry them from there to EQUANCOURT. One limber for "D" & "C" Coys. will be at "D" Coy. Hdqrs., and one limber for "B" & "A" Coys., and one limber for Battn. Hdqrs will be at COSEY COPSE at 5.30 pm.

In The Field.   (sd) G. Reeve, Lt. & Asst. Adj.
3. 10. 17.   1st Battn. Royal Irish Fusiliers.

Operations Order
By
Major, S.U.L. Clements
Commanding 1st Battalion Royal Irish Fusiliers.
Field 8-10-17.

---

(1) Relief. The Battalion will relieve the 10th R.I.Rifles in the line to-morrow night. The disposition of the Battn. in the line will be as follows:-

"D" Company.   Right Company.
"A" Company.   Centre Company.
"B" Company.   Left Company.
"C" Company.   Reserve.

An advance Party consisting of one Officers and two N.C.O'S per Coy. will parade at 2-15 p.m. and will proceed to trenches to take over stores etc., Companies will make their own arrangements with Coys. of R.I.R. ref. Guides if any are required.
Battn. will parade in Camp at 5p.m. and will march to entrain at P.29.c. at 6p.m. for TRESCAULT.
2/Lt. H.S. Lee will act as entraining Officer and will report to 9th Light Railway Company. at 5-30p.m.
1 Marker per Company will report to the R.S.M. at 4-55.
List of trench stores taken over will be sent to Battn. H.Qrs, by 11a.m. 10th inst.
Order of march H.Qrs. "D" "A" "B" "C".
Returns to bre rendered while in the trenches will be the same as for last tour i.e.
Situation Reports 3a.m. & 3p.m.
Intelligence and Casualty Reports 9-15 a.m.
Pro-formas for Intelligence and Patrol Reports arec issued to all concerned.with Battn. Orders.

Companies will report " RELIEF COMPLETE" to Battn. H.Qrs. by Orderly.

(2) Details. All details other than Regt. Transport and Q.Mr. Staff will M.C. parade with Battn. and will proceed to METZ under 2/Lt. T. Houston/ This Party will be billetted in METZ.

(3) Transport. All articles for transport will be ready at 4-15p.m.
Blankets will be rolled in bundles of ten securely tied, labelled, and stacked outside "C" Company's line at 2p.m.

(4) Packs. The wearing of packs up to the line is optional and Coy's not wishing to take them to the line will have them stacked with their Blankets as per above.

(5) Trench Wardens. 1 N.C.O. and 10 men (trench wardens) of "D" Coy. will parade at 2-30p.m. and proceed and report to O.C. Trench Wardens HAVRINCOURT HAVRINCOURT WOOD.

(6) Inspection. The Commanding Officer will inspect Company Lines at 4-30p.m.

Lieut. & A/Adjt.
1st Battalion Royal Irish Fusiliers.

Operation Order
by
Major, S.U.L. Clements
Commanding, 1st Battn. Royal Irish Fusiliers.

(1) Relief. The Battalion will be relieved by the 10th R.I.R. to-morrow night, and on relief will proceed to METZ, Companies taking over the same as for last tour in METZ The 10th R.I.R. leave METZ about 6 pm.
Reports on "Work completed" and "Work in hand" to reach Battalion Hdqrs. by 9.15 am. Lists of stores to be handed over, and lists of stores taken over in METZ will be handed in at Battn. Hdqrs by 12 noon on the 16th inst.

(2) Adv. Party. One officer and one N.C.O. from each Company and Battn. Hdqrs.; will report during the day and take over billets etc.; work been carried on by the 10th R.I.R. will also be taken over.

(3) Water Tins. Companies will bring out all water tins and on arrival at Metz will hand them over to the detachment of R.A.M.C attached to the Battn.

(4) Ammunition. All N.C.O's and men will be made up with the correct ammount of S.A.A. before leaving the line. A report will be furnished by 9 am. on the 20th inst. to the effect that all ranks are complete in S.A.A. according to War Establishment.

(5) Transport. One Limber each for "C" & "D" Coys.; will be at "C" Coys.; Hdqrs at TRESCAULT at 8.15 pm. One limber each for Battn. Hdqrs.; "B" & "A" Coys.; will be at Battn.; Hdqrs.; at 8.45 pm.

In The Field.   (sd) G. Reeve. Lt. & A/Adjt.
14.10.17.   1st Battn. Royal Irish Fusiliers.

Operation Orders
by
Major S. J. L. **LEMETTS**.,
Commanding 1st Battalion Royal Irish Fusiliers.,
In the Field, 20-10-17.

:*:

1. Duties Officers.
    Battalion Orderly Officer tomorrow :- 2/Lieut. G.C.WATSON.

2. Divine Service.
    Divine Service tomorrow will be as under :-
    C.of E. Parade Service. Companies will parade under the senior officer on parade, on LEICESTER SQUARE, at 10-50 a.m. for service in BAROSSA HALL at 11-0 a.m. 1 Officer per Coy. and Bn.H².Qrs. will attend.
    C.of E. Voluntary Service. Holy Communion at 8-30 a.m. and 11-45 a Evening Prayer at 5-0 p.m.

    R.C.Parade Service. Coys. will parade under 2/Lieut. J.M.O'DRISCOLL on LEICESTER SQUARE at 9-50 a.m. for service in BAROSSA HALL at 10-0 a.m.
    R.C.Voluntary Service. Rosary in R.C.Chaplain's billet at 4- p.m.

    Presbyterians Parade Service. Coys. will parade on LEICESTER SQ. at 9-45 a.m. and will march to the little church, METZ for service at 10-0 a.m. The Senior N.C.O. present will take charge of the parade.

    Right Markers for parade services will report to the R.S.M. on the parade ground 5 minutes before hour of parade.

3. Roll Call.
    C.O's Roll Call will be at :-   8-0 a.m.

4. Office.
    C.O's Office will be at :-   12 noon.

5. Sick.
    Sick Parade will be at :-   8-30 a.m.

6. Relief.
    The Battn. will relieve the 10th Battn. Roy.Ir.Rifles in the line tomorrow. Disposition of Coys. in the line will be as follows :- "C" Right Coy, "A" Centre Coy., "B" Left Coy., "D" Reserve.
    Advance Party. 1 Officer and 2 N.J.O's per Coy. will parade at the Orderly Room at 2-15 p.m. and proceed to the trenches and take over stores etc.
    Order of March to the Trenches.   H².Qrs.,B,C,A,D.Coys.
    Leading Coy will move at 5-40 p.m.   10 minutes between Coys. 100 yards between pln. comn.
    Transport. 1 Limber will report to Bn.H².Qrs. and each Coy at 5-0 p.m. also 1 Limber will report at above for "A" and "C" Coys. cooks and 1 Limber for "B" and "D" Coy. Cooks.
    All bags, trench stores etc. will be taken over and a list sent to Bn.H².Qrs. by 10-0 a.m. on the 22nd inst.
    Coys. will report relief complete by orderly.
    Lists of stores,Tents,Huts etc to be handed over will be sent to the Orderly Room by 12 noon tomorrow.
    The Orderly Room, Drums, and 2 Pioneers will remain with 2/Lieut. T.HOUSTON...J. at old Bn. H².Qrs.
    Packs. Coys. not wishing to take packs into the line, will store them in METZ under Coy arrangements.
    Intelligence and Patrol Reports will be sent so as to reach Bn. H².Qrs. by 7-0 a.m. daily.

                                                    P.T.O.

7. **Lewis Gun Class.**
   A man per Coy will be detailed to remain at MTC to undergo course of instruction under 2/Lieut. T. HOUSTON, M.G.

8. **Stores etc. (Salvage)**
   All ranks can help considerably in maintaining the necessary supplies of clothing and equipment required by the Army by salving and returning to stores every article they can find, no matter how small nor in what condition.
   Owing to the difficulty of getting stores at home, the authorities are asking that this may be done and all ranks are requested to help. Salved articles can always be sent to the Qr.Mr. by returning ration limbers or train.

9. **Socks.**
   When the Battn. is in the Line, all wet socks will be sent to Battn. H.Qrs. and a receipt will be given for same by Corpl. of the R.A.M.C. who will have the socks dried and returned to Coys. When the socks require washing or exchange they will be brought by C.Q.M.S's to the Qr.Mr. who will exchange them.

10. **Bolt Covers.**
    Bolt covers will always be used on rifles except when troops are on Sentry.

11. **Revetments.**
    Owing to the large demands on the supply of corrugated iron for hutting and horse standings, etc. the practice of using it for revetting purposes in the trenches must cease.

12. **Working Parties (Tools).**
    Cases have occurred in which working parties have thrown ~~XXXXXXXXXXXXXXXXXX~~ down their tools carelessly in the locality in which they had been working, on the completion of their task. Officers and N.C.O's in charge of parties will be warned that all tools must be returned to, and properly stacked in, the dumps from which they were drawn, and any slackness in carrying out this order will be punished by disciplinary action.

13. **Box Respirators.**
    When it is necessary for men carrying rifles to put on their small box respirators, they should be instructed to hold their rifles between their knees (as when unfixing bayonets), whilst adjusting their respirators.

             G. Reid Lieut. and Asst. Adjt.
             1st Battalion Royal Irish Fusiliers.

Operation Orders
by
Major. S.U.L. Clements
Commanding, 1st Battn. Royal Irish Fusiliers

(1) Relief. The Battalion will be relieved by the 10th R.I.R. and on relief will marcd to TRESCAULT railhead to entrain for EQUANCOURT. 2/Lt. E.J. PARKHILL will act as entraining officer.

Companies will report "Relief complete" by orderly.

(2) Stores. List of trench stores to be handed over to be sent to Battn. Hdqrs by 9 am. to-morrow.
Great care to be taken that lists of stores are accurate as many errors have been made during the last two tours.

"Work completed" and "Work in hand" report to reach Battn. Hdqrs to reach by 11 am. to-morrow.

(3) Adv. Party. One N.C.O. per Coy. will parade at PLACE MORTMERE at 2 pm. an proceed and report to Capt. W. Scott at EQUANCOURT at 3.30 pm.

(4) Detached Parties. Bde Works party, Trench Wardens, and Cable Party will rejoin Coys. to-morrow evenng at EQUANCOURT and will remain with Coys. during tour in billets at that place

(5) Lewis Guns. All Lewis Guns will be taken in train limbers wall meet train at Q.M. Stores to carry them from there to EQUANCOURT One limber for "D" & "C" Companies will be at "D" Coys. Hdqrs. and one limber for "B" & "A" Coy and one for Battn. Hdqrs will be at COSEY COPSE at 5.30. pm.

In The Field.   (sd) G. Reeve. Lt. & A/Adjt.
26. 10. 17.   1st Battn. Royal Irish Fusiliers.

C O N F I D E N T I A L.

WAR DIARY

OF

1st. BATTALION ROYAL IRISH FUSILIERS.

FROM. 1-11-1917

TO 30-11-1917.

M.J. Furnell
Lieut.Colonel,
Commanding 1st Battalion Royal Irish Fusiliers.

Field,
3-12-17.

SECRET.   Copy No.

Preliminary Instruction No.10.

1. ZERO HOUR is 6-20 a.m.
2. Breakfasts will be at 5-30 a.m.
3. Officers Valices will be stacked outside the Orderly Room at 6-0 a.m.
4. Right Markers will report to the R.S.M. at 6-30 a.m.
5. The Battalion will parade at 6-35 a.m., March off from camp at 6-45 a.m. and pass starting point at 7-5 a.m.

6. 2 O.R's "C" Coy. (Brigade Intelligence Party), will now report at 8-30 a.m.

7. On arrival at Assembly Positions, Coys. will immediately draw stores and will report to Battn. Hd.Qrs. as soon as all are ready to move.

8. 1 N.C.O. per Coy. also 4 Orderlies already detailed, who will act as an Advance Party to HINDENBURG SYSTEM, under Lieut. G.C. WATSON, will report to him at the Orderly Room at 6-30 a.m. tomorrow. This Party will report to the Adjutant tonight at 7-30 p.m. for 2 rolls of tracing tape.

9. Soup will not now be served but dinners will be served at about 9-0 a.m.

Field,   Captain and Adjutant
15-11-17   1st Battalion Royal Irish Fusiliers.

Army Form C. 2118.

WAR DIARY
or
INTELLIGENCE SUMMARY.

(Erase heading not required.)

Instructions regarding War Diaries and Intelligence Summaries are contained in F. S. Regs., Part II. and the Staff Manual respectively. Title pages will be prepared in manuscript.

Place	Date	Hour	Summary of Events and Information	Remarks and references to Appendices
In the Field.	1-11-17.		Battn. worked on new Camp all day, building cookhouses and fire places. Weather fine. Captain W.A.FOLEY died of wounds at 48 C.C.S.	Rept.
	2-11-17.		Weather dull. Battn. worked during the morning on improvements to camp. Funeral service was held at 48 C.C.S. for the late Captain W.A.FOLEY. 15 Officers and 50 O.R's and the Drums attended. Map location of grave yard (Sheet 57c V.2.a.9.3. His death was deeply regretted throughout the Battn. The Battn. relieved 10th Roy.Ir.Rifles in the line and proceeded to the trenches by train. Relief complete 8-0 p.m. Enemy guns were very active and caught relieved troops on their way out. 1 prisoner of 84 I.R. taken by "G" Coy. Prisoner died before reaching Field Ambulance. He was one of a patrol who tried to bomb a post.	Rept. See appx. "A"
	3-11-17		(omitted in diary for Oct.25th.) G.S.M.CULLEN and Sergt.Nicholson, granted commissions and gazetted to this Battn. as 2/Lieuts. Weather dull and misty. Our patrols were active. Enemy Artillery active at night on Ration Dump 7 Men wounded. November 4th.	Rept.
	4-11-17		Weather dull and Misty. Works started on Support Line which had to be completed in 4 days. Enemy Artillery again active on ration dump at night. 1 man wounded.	Rept.
	5-11-17		Weather dull and Misty. Ordinary Trench Work continued. Gap was blown in Enemy wire with amon ammonal tube. The death sentance on No.12609 Pte. G.HANNA was promulgated at BARROSA HALL METZ by Captain and Adjutant W.SCOTT,M.C. This was the first death sentence ordered to be carried out in this Battn. since its arrival in France. Pte.Hanna was only about 5 Hours with the Battn. He having joined with a draft but when warned for the trenches, disappeared. Firing Party, under Lieut. G.REEVE,M.C. proceeded to Divnl. Hd.Qrs.	Rept.
	6-11-17		Weather dull and wet. Work continued. Pte.Hanna shot at 6-40 a.m. Trial of 2/Lieut.P.G.H. MANSFIELD, commenced by General Court Martial, commenced. The following officers joined the Battn. 2/Lieuts. G.SHERSBY, E.A.SIMPSON, R.M.MOORE, G.W.R.TEMPLAR, E.J.HARRISON, T.S.HASWELL, D.O'TOOLE.	Appx.
	7-11-17		Weather wet in morning, fine towards evening. Work continued. Battn.relieved by 10th R.Ir.Rifles. Rept + on relief proceeded to Billets in METZ.	See APPX "B"

A.5834 Wt. W4973/M687 750,000 8/16 D. D. & L. Ltd. Forms/C.2118/13.

Army Form C. 2118.

WAR DIARY
or
INTELLIGENCE SUMMARY.
(Erase heading not required.)

Instructions regarding War Diaries and Intelligence Summaries are contained in F.S. Regs., Part II. and the Staff Manual respectively. Title pages will be prepared in manuscript.

Hour, Date, Place	Summary of Events and Information	Remarks and references to Appendices
In the Field		
8-11-17.	Weather wet. Battalion bathed and cleaned up, found working parties in the afternoon and evening.	J.G.
9-11-17.	Working parties for whole Battalion.	J.G.
10-11-17	As for 9th.	J.G.
11-11-17	As for 9th. Weather wet.	J.G.
12-11-17	As for 9th.	J.G.
13-11-17	2/Lieuts. R.E.GLOVER and B.HARTLEY joined the Battalion. The Battalion relieved the 10th Roy. Irish Rifles in the Line. Relief complete 7-30 p.m. The Battn. subsequently relieved the 8/9th Royal Irish Rifles of a portion of their line to "B" Sap inclusive. Quiet night.	J.G. See Appx."C"
14-11-17.	Weather fine but misty. Quiet day. The C.O. and Intelligence Officer proceeded to DEMICOURT to view Enemy trenches from that sector.	J.G.
15-11-17	Weather fine but less misty. 2nd in Command, Adjutant and O.C's "C" and "D" Coys. proceeded to DEMICOURT to view Enemy trenches. Working parties furnished for the completion of Duckboards and trench ladders.	J.G.
16-11-17	Weather fine. Enemy Artillery more active than usual. Party (same as for 15th) proceeded to DEMICOURT. O.C's "B" and "A" Coy's and 2 N.C.O's per Coy.and Bn.Intelligence Officer.	J.G.
17&11-17	Battalion relieved in front line by the 2/7th WEST YORKS. Bn.Hd.Qrs.relieved by 18.5 Infantry Brigade. Relief complete 10-30 p.m. Battn. left 11 O.R's in each of the saps "B","C","D","E" and in "MONS Post". Battn. moved to Billets in METZ. Day fine. Enemy artillery normal.	J.G. See Appx."D"
18-11-17	Weather fine. At 5-30 a.m. the enemy, after a night in which persistant efforts had been made to cut our wire round "E" Sap succeeded in rushing 1 post. 6 of our men are missing. The enemy's previous attempts had been driven off by our bombers but on this occasion he put down a BOX barrage of trench mortars etc. and succeeded in entering the Sap under cover of the noise and rushing the Right hand post.	J.G.

WAR DIARY
or
INTELLIGENCE SUMMARY.
(Erase heading not required.)

Army Form C. 2118.

Place	Date	Hour	Summary of Events and Information	Remarks and references to Appendices
In the Field	18-11-17		Battalion moved into Billets near YTRES starting 5-15 p.m.	See Appx. E
	19-11-17.		Weather fine. Surplus kits packed. Final orders issued for move forward.	
	20-11-17.		Battn. paraded 7-5 a.m. and moved from YTRES camp 450 strong to preliminary assembly position at "SPOIL HEAP" (J.34.c.80.25.) ref. map 57 c N.W. Battn. had dinners at 1-30 p.m. before moving to vicinity of SQUARE COPSE (K.25.d.50.70.) and remained in open field until 7-30 p.m. Battn. then moved in rear of Brigade accross a bridge in single file to HAVRINCOURT and took 7½ hours to made the journey, a distance of 2 Miles, owing to road difficulties. Battn. were billetted in German trenches West of HAVRINCOURT. Very wet night. Lieut.Colonel M.J.FURNELL joined to take over command of the Battn. and remained with the details.	
	21-11-17.		Weather dull. Rain from 6-0 p.m. Battn. arrived about 3 to 3-30 a.m. at German trenches WEST of HAVRINCOURT and were up again at 8-0 a.m. The Battn. left trenches, marching in rear of the Brigade at 3-45 p.m. to trenches in K.10.d. (Part of HINDENBURG Support) West of HAVRINCOURT, and arrived about 8-0 p.m. The Battn. in front lost its way and it became necessary to march by compass.	
	22-11-17		Weather fine. Battn. moved in Artillery formation at 11=0 a.m. to trenches vacated by 10th R.I.R. (in K.4.b.) who had gone into action. At 7-0 p.m. the Battalion moved forward and occupied line of trenches North of the BAPAUME – CAMBRAI Road in E.27.b.	
	23-11-17		Weather fine. At 12-10 p.m. the Battn. were ordered into Assemble Positions to take part in a second phase of the attack which started at 10-30 a.m. On coming out of trenches, the Battn. came under heavy Machine Gun fire. It was reported by a tank that a strong point erect* on the road to the assembly position had not fallen. It To reach assembly position it was necessary to take this. It was therefore attacked. The Battn. sustained the following casualties :- 8 Officers and 225 O.R's and got as far as the German wire of the main position with 3 Officers and 30 O.R's including 6 wounded. The assemble position was not taken. Battn. were then advanced to ROUND trench, the Strong Point and No.5 LOCK on the canal. Battn. were relieved by the 10th Roy.Irish Rifles and 8/9th Roy.Irish Rifles in Round Trench and No.5 Lock respectively, about 10-0 p.m. Lieut.Colonel S.U.L.CLEMENTS was slightly wounded but remained at duty.	
	24-11-17.		At 1-0 p.m. Battn. moved t trenches in E.22.a. and relieved 15th R.Ir.Rifles and prepared for an attack at 3-30 p.m. after a bombardment of heavies starting at 3-10 p.m. The attack was the first phase of the battle on the 23rd November.	

Army Form C. 2118.

WAR DIARY
or
INTELLIGENCE SUMMARY.
(Erase heading not required.)

Instructions regarding War Diaries and Intelligence Summaries are contained in F. S. Regs., Part II. and the Staff Manual respectively. Title pages will be prepared in manuscript.

Place	Date	Hour	Summary of Events and Information	Remarks and references to Appendices
In the Field	24-11-17		Artillery Barrage started on early but did not ××××××× have desired effect, the battn. sustaining 22 casualties from our own barrage. Bombardment continued North and East of the trenches we were to attack for 40 minutes after the Battalion was due to go over. It was decided by a senior Coy.Commander that it was useless to go over. The strongpoints which were to be taken West of the Assembly position were not touched.	See Appx. "F".
	25-11-17		Weather wet. Trenches improved by being deepened 2 feet which made them safe for one to walk along without being hit.	
	26-11-17		Battalion relieved by 1 Coy. 1st K.R.R.C. and on relief moved to the SLAG HEAP, North of HERMIES WEST of the canal. Filthy night - sleet and wind. Battn. arrived at SLAG HEAP at about 4-0 a.m. Throughout 20th and to 26th November, 2/Lieut.G.G.WATSON and Rev.F.DONOHUE did splendid work; 2/Lieut.Watson in his untiring energy in reconnoitring and reporting on positions and his disregard for his own personal safety and his self sacrifice. Father Donohue in going round the line at all times and under very trying circumstances did much to keep up the moral and spirits of the Battn.	
	27-11-17		Weather fine. Battn. moved at 4-0 p.m. from SLAG HEAP, North of HERMIES to Camp at BARASTRE arriving there at 7-45 p.m. 2/Lieut.D.O'TOOLE who was wounded on 23rd was reported as having died of wounds.	
	28-11-17		Bn. remained in BARASTRE camp. Weather Fine. Day spent in cleaning up, taking lists of deficiencies.	See Appx. "G"
	29-11-17		Weather fine. Battn. entrained at YTRES at 9-45 a.m. for REVIERE (Ref.sheet LENS 11) and arrived in Billets at BERNAVILLE about 2-0 p.m.	
	30-11-17		Weather fine. Day spent in cleaning up and taking lists of deficiencies etc.	
	3-11-17		(October 30th) Letter received from Brig.Genl.R.J.KENTISH,D.S.O., congratulating All ranks of Battn. on state of Battn. during his visit.	See Appx. "H"

M.F. Purnell
Lieut.Colonel,
Commanding 1st Battalion Royal Irish Fusiliers.

Battalion Orders
By
Lieut.Colonel S. U. L. C L E M E N T S.,
Commanding 1st Battalion Royal Irish Fusiliers.,

Field, 1-11-17.

The Battn. will relieve the 10th R.Ir.Rifles in the line tomorrow night.
Disposition of the Battn. in the line will be as follows :-
Right Coy "C", Centre Coy. "D", Left Coy. "B", Reserve Coy."A".
The Battn. will entrain for renches at 5-0 p.m. at P.32.b.5.5.
Order of March, Hd.Qrs., C,B,D,A.Coys.
The Battn. will parade on ground near Officers Lines at 4-30 p.m.
1 Marker per Coy and Bn.Hd.Qrs. will report to the R.S.M. at 4-25 p.m.
<u>Advance Party.</u> 1 Officer and 2 N.C.O's per Coy. and Bn.Hd.Qrs. will
proceed to the trenches to take over stores etc. at 1-0 p.m.
2/Lieut.E.J.PARKHILL is detailed entraining officer and will arrange
for trains etc direct with No.0 L.O.R.C., R.E. at entraining point by 1p.m.
All articles for transport will be ready by 3-45 p.m.

(sd) L.Scott
Captain and Adjutant,
1st Battalion Royal Irish Fusiliers....

Battalion Orders
By
Lieut.Colonel S. U. L. C L E M E N T S.,
Commanding 1st Battalion Royal Irish Fusiliers.,
Field, 6-11-17.

1. Relief.

The Battalion will be relieved tomorrow night and by the 10th R.Ir. Rifles and on relief will proceed to Billets in METZ.

Advance Party. 1 Officer Hd.Qrs. and 2 N.C.O's per Coy will proceed to METZ during the morning and take over.

Lists of stores to be handed over will be sent to Bn.Hd.Qrs. by 11-a.m. 7th inst. and Lists of stores taken over from 10th R.Ir.Rifles will be sent to the Order,y Room by 2-0 p.m. 8th inst.

All limbers etc., except 1 for the cooks which will arrive as soon as possible after dark, will arrive at Bn. Hd.Qrs. at about 6-30 p.m.

(Sd) L. Scott   Captain and Adjutant,
1st Battalion Royal Irish Fusiliers.

Battalion Orders
By
Lieut.Colonel S. U. L. C L E M E N T S.,
Commanding 1st Battalion Royal Irish Fusiliers.,
Field, 12-11-17.

Relief.

The Battn. will relieve the 10th R.Ir.Rifles in the line tomorrow night
Advance Party consisting of 1 Officer and 1 N.C.O per Coy and Bn. Hd.
Qrs. will proceed to the line during the morning and take over.
Disposition in the line will be :- Right Coy."C" Centre Coy "D"
Left Coy "A", Reserve Coy "B".
Lists of stores taken over will be sent to Bn.Hd.Qrs. by 11-a.m. 14th ins
Transport to take stores etc to the line will arrive at Bn.Hd.Qrs.
at 3-45 p.m.
Order of March to the Trenches :- Hd.Qrs., C.A.D.B.Coys.
All blankets and Officers Kits will be ready by 1-30 p.m.
Coys will report relief complete by orderly.

Captain and Adjutant,
1st Battalion Royal Irish Fusiliers.

Operation Orders
by
Lieut. Col. S.U.L. Clements.,
Commanding 1st Battalion Royal Irish Fusiliers.

In the Field, 16/11/17.

1. **Relief.**
The Battalion, less Outpost Line, will be relieved on night of 17th/18th, inst. by the 2/7th WEST YORKS REGIMENT.
The Battn. will leave 1 N.C.O. and 10 men in each Sap and in Mons Post
No Lewis Guns will be left behind.
"B" Coy. will supply garrison for "B" Sap.
"C" "   "   "   "   " "C" "
"D" "   "   "   "   " "D" and "E" Saps.
"A" "   "   "   "   " "Mons Post"

The following Officers will remain in the Line:-
Lieut. E.H. Verdon, 2/Lt. A. Joules, 2/Lt. R.H. Moore, undrer the Ord orders of Lieut. E.H. Verdon, who will report to Battn. H.Qrs., to-night for instructions. Two days rations, water and solidified alch alchohol will come up for these garrisons on night of 17th inst., and will be carried to posts by "D" Coy.
6 Water tins will be kept by each Sap and Post, these will be brought to "B" Coy's H.Qrs., TRESCAULT at 6 p.m. 17th.
Men who bring tins will act as Guides to posts. Ration arrive at 3 p.m. Garrisons of Posts, on being relieved at daylight on 19th inst. will bring water tins with them.

Garrisons of MONS POST will evacuate their post just before daylight on 19th inst. Garrisons will evacuate B,C,D, and E, Saps just after daylight on 19th inst.
On evacuation of Posts all garrisons will report to Lieut. E.H. Verdon at our present Battn. H.Qrs. The party will then march to PLACE MORTEMARE.   where G.S. Waggons will be waiting to convey them to the Battn. at 7 a.m.

Posts may retain Gumboots if required but will bring them out with them on 19th inst., hand them over to N.C.O. i/c Gumboot Store in HAVRINCOURT WOOD and obtain receipt for them.

Disposition of the 2/7th Westv Yorks Regt. on taking over will be as follows:-
"C" Coy (W.Y's) from "B" Sap to "D" Sap.
"B" "   "   "   " "D" Sap " SHROPSHIRE ROAD inclusive.
"A" "   "   "   "   SHROPSHIRE ROAD inclusive to junction
communication Trench between Front and Support Lines in Q.3.a.7.2.
"D" Coy. (W.Y's) 1 Platoon from Q.3.a.7.2. to OXFORD ROAD, 2 Platoons in support.
The Coy's of the 2/7th West Yorks Regt. consists of 3 platoons.
Companies will divide up Coy. frontagees to suit the West Yorks.

Guides.
All guides will report to 2/Lt. G.C. Watson at PLACE MORTEMARE 5-15 on 17th inst. They will be in possession of a piece of paper showing Coy. and Platoon of the West Yorks they are guides for.

"C" Coy. will provide 4 guides viz:- 1 per platoon for "C" Coy. (W.Y' Right, Centre, and Left Platoons and 1 for Coy. H.Qrs. which goes into our Right Coy. H.Qrs.

"D" Coy. will provide 4 guides viz:- 1 per Platoon for "C" Coy. (W.Y's Right, Centre, and Left Platoons & 1 for Coy. H.Qrs. which goes inton our Right Coy. H.Qrs.

Sheet 2.

"A" Coy. will provide 6 guides for "A" and "B" Coy's West Yorks Regt.
    viz:- 1 per Platoon for "A" Coy. (W.Y's) Right, Centre, and
        Left Platoons.
        1 for te Platoon of "B" Coy. (W.Y's) for the "Front Line"
        1 each per Coy. H.Qrs. "A" & "B" Coy's who go into our
        Left Coy. H.Qrs.

Bn. H.Qrs. will provide 3 guides viz:-
        1 each per 2 Platoons "B" Coy. (W.Y's) for Support Line.
        1 for Bn. H.Qrs. (W.Y's) which goes into No 75 Dugout,
        (our Centre Coy. H.Qrs.)

        ****

Part of "B" Coy. in TRESCAULT and Cosy Copse can move as soon as rations are delivered to Saps.

The Battalion on relief will move to Billets in METZ and will move to LECHELLE Area on morning of the 18th inst.
Transport will arrive at Bn. H.Qrs. at 6-30 p.m.
Water tins (less 6 per Saps and post) and Food Containers, will be brought out of the Line.

Lists of Stores to be handed over, will be sent to Bn. H.Qrs. by 11 a.m. 17th inst. (Stores between Q.3.a.7.2. and Oxford Road will be handed over to "A" Coy. West Yorks Regt.)

Receipts for Stores handed over will be sent to Bn. H.Qrs., when sending "Relief Complete" reports. No "Work" reports are required.

"C" Coy's Cooks will come out of the Line with the Battalion.
Men i/c of Gumboot Store, and Brigade Grenade Guard, will rejoin their respective Coy's on night of 17th inst.
Regulations ref. Traffic, issued on the 13th inst., will be strictly observed

Advance Party.
1 Officer and 1 N.C.O. per Coy. and Bn. H.Qrs. will report at 1-30 p.m. on 17th inst., to the Town Major, METZ. for Billets.
Coy's will report "Relief Complete" by Orderly.

        (sgd) W.Scott, M.C. Capt. and Adjutant.
      1st Battalion Royal Irish Fusiliers.

Battalion Orders
By
Lieut.Colonel S. U. L. C L E M E N T S.,
Commanding 1st Battalion Royal Irish Fusiliers.,
Field, 18-11-17.

1. MOVE. The Battn. will move to tents in P.26.a. near YTRES today starting at 5-15 p.m.
Order of March :- Hd.Qrs., C.A.B.D.Coys.

Transport. A Motor Lorry will arrive at about 12 Noon. Any coys who have stores etc and wish to send them on this lorry will have them stacked outside the Orderly Room at above hour. Officers valices and remainder of articles for transport will be ready by 12 noon.

Captain and Adjutant,
1st Battalion Royal Irish Fusiliers.

Appendix "F"

SECRET.   Copy No.

Preliminary Instruction No.2.

1. **Orderlies.**
   The following will be attached to the Brigade Hd.Qrs. as Orderlies, reporting on the 14th Inst., rationed up to the 16th inst. inclusive:-
   L.Cpl.Brady, Ptes.Plowman, Walsh, McCarten, (Drums).
   They will be fully equipped with rifles, Blankets etc.
   "D" Coy. will detail 1 Lewis Gunner to be attached to Hd.Qrs. as a runner and to help fill Lewis Gun Magazines at Bn.Hd.Qrs. in the event of ammunition being available there. He will report today.
   "A", "B" and "C" Coys. will each detail 1 intelligent Other rank to report to Bn.Hd.Qrs. today, as orderly.
   The following men from the drums will join Bn. Hd.Qrs. as runners today:-
   Ptes. McMullen, Woods and Maloney.

2. **Signallers.**
   3 Signallers will be attached to Bde.Hd.Qrs. and will report there by 10-0 a.m. on the 14th inst rationed for the 15th inst and fully equipped.

3. **Loaders.**
   1 Man each from "A", "B" and "C" Coys together with remainder of drummers under the Drum Major, will report to the Transport Officer today rationed up to the 14th inst. They will be employed as loaders under the T.Offr.

   2 O.R. from "D" Coy. will be employed as loaders with 107th M.G.Coy. and will report to the Transport Lines of that unit by 4-0 p.m. today.

4. **Stretcher Bearers.**
   4 Additional Men per Coy will be employed as Stretcher Bearers.
   2 of these per Coy. will report to the M.O. in the line daily at 10-0 a.m and the other 2 at 2-0 p.m. starting from tomorrow.

5. **Trench Wardens.**
   The Trench Wardens of "D" Coy will remain under Lieut.W.D.BRADLEY and will act as Bn.Carriers.

6. **R. E's.**
   Coys. will hold men, as under, in readiness to be attached to the R.E's:-
   "A" Coy. 7, "B" Coy. 7, "C" Coy. 6, and "D" Coy. 6.

Field,   Captain and Adjutant
13-11-17   1st Battalion Royal Irish Fusiliers.

LIST OF APPENDIXES.

Index Letter.	Purport.	Remarks.
"A"	Battn. Orders.- Relief of 10th R.Ir.Rifles in the Line by the Battn.	
"B"	Battn. relieved in the line by the 10th R.Ir.Rifles. Bn.Orders	
"C"	Battn. relieve 10th R.Ir.Rifles in the Line. Bn. Orders.	
"D"	Battn.Order. - Battn. relieved in the line by the 2/7th WEST YORKS Regt.	
"E"	Battn.Orders.- Battj. move to tents near YTRES (P.WY.a.).	
"F"	Preliminary Instructions for attack on BOURLON WOOD etc.	
"G"	Battn. Orders. - Battn. entrain at YTRES for FOSSEUX (training) Area.	
"H"	Letter of congratulation on state of the Battn. at time of his visit, from Brig.Genl. R.J.KENTISH,D.S.O.	

Field,
3-12-17.

M.J. Farrell Lieut.Colonel,

Commanding 1st Battalion Royal Irish Fusiliers.

SECRET.

Preliminary Instructions No 4

(1) **Formation for attack.**

Herewith sketches of Coy. and Battn. formations for attack. These cancel previous instructions.

(2) **On Z plus 1 day.**

Battalion will be on a two Coy. front, each Coy. on 3 Platoon basis. Battn. front 400 yards. Coy. front 200 yards. Platoon front 100 yards.
"D" Coy. will be right front   "B" Coy. left front
"A" "   "   "   Support "C" "   " Support

1st wave of each Coy will be on a two Platoon front 3rd Platoon acting as moppers up.
3rd Platoon of support coy. will form 3rd wave and will act as a support to the other two Platoons.
Sections will advance in column until forced to extend.

The interval between lines will be 20 yards and will be 70 yards between waves.
Moppers up will follow 1st wave at intervals of 15 yards.

Suggested positions of Sections as in Sketch.
Lewis Gun Sections will always be on outer flank of second lines. Fourth Lewis Gun of each Coy. will be in centre of Coy. under the Company Commander.

(3) **Maps.**

The following maps will be carried by all officers and will be referred to in all orders and messages:-
    57 C. N.E.
    51 B. S.E.
NOEUVRES sheets will be carried by N.C.O's.

(4) **S.O.S.**

Cavalry	1" the GREEN Very Light
III Corps	R.G. bursting into 2 Green & 2 WHITE
IVth Corps	R.G. " " 2 Red & 2 WHITE
Vth Corps	R.G. " " 2 RE & 2 GREEN

(5) **Flares.**

Cavalry use RE flares. Infantry use WHITE flares.

(6) **Casualties.**

Casualty Reports will be rendered as follows:-
(a) Daily casualty wire covering period up to wiring to reach Batt. Hqrs. by 1 pm. This wire will give names of Officers and O.R's, date of their casualty, nature of casualty, under headings:- Killed, Wounded, Missing, Missing believe Killed, Missing believe Wounded and wounded and Missing.
(b) As soon as possible after action an estimate of No's of Other Ranks casualties and name and nature of officers casualties as far as is possible will be sent to Battn. Hqrs.
This will be rendered daily, the total No. of casualties only to be given i.e.
    Oct. 20th   Estimate   casualties   45 O.R's.
    Oct. 21st   "   "   47 O.R's.
    Oct. 22nd   "   "   89 O.R's
This means that two casualties had occured since report rendered on 20th Oct. and 42 casualties had occured since report rendered for 20-21st Oct.

Field. 15/11/17   Captain & Adjutant.

```
1st Coy  ⎧  ^20"        R☐    B☐    R☐    B☐           ⎫ 1st LINE ⎫
         ⎨  x           ☐LG   ②     ☐RG         R☐G    ① LG☐    ⎬         ⎬ 1st WAVE
         ⎩  15"v              |/    B☐    LG☐ ③  RG☐    R☐        ⎭ 2nd LINE⎭
              <— 100" — x — 100" —>                                      Moppers up

         70"    Note: Coys in 1st wave of assaulting Bns will send forward
                      2 Rifle Sections as Scouts replacing them with 2 L.G.
                      Sections from No 3 Platoon.

2nd Coy  ⎧  ^25"         R☐    B☐    R☐    B☐           ⎫ 1st Line ⎫
         ⎨  x LG☐        ②     RG☐         RG☐    ①  LG☐          ⎬ 2nd Line ⎬ 2nd Wave
         ⎩  10"v               |/    B☐    ③ R☐           RG☐       ⎭          ⎭
              ↓
                         B☐                                                ⎫ 3rd Wave
                              LG☐                 RG☐                      ⎬ Supports
                                                                           ⎭ 1 Pl. of 2nd Coy
```

"A" Form
MESSAGES AND SIGNALS.

Army Form C. 2121
(in pads of 100).

No. of Message..................

Prefix............Code............m.	Words.	Charge.	This message is on a/c of:	Recd. at...........m.
Office of Origin and Service Instructions.	Sent			
....	At............m.		.....................Service.	Date ....
....	To............			From ....
....	By............		(Signature of "Franking Officer.")	By............

TO {

*	Sender's Number.	Day of Month.	In reply to Number.	**A A A**

From			
Place			
Time			

The above may be forwarded as now corrected. **(Z)**

....
Censor.   Signature of Addressor or person authorised to telegraph in his name.

*This line should be erased if not required.

(18965.) Wt. W12952/M1294. 187,500 Pads. 1/17 McC. & Co., Ltd. (E. 818.)

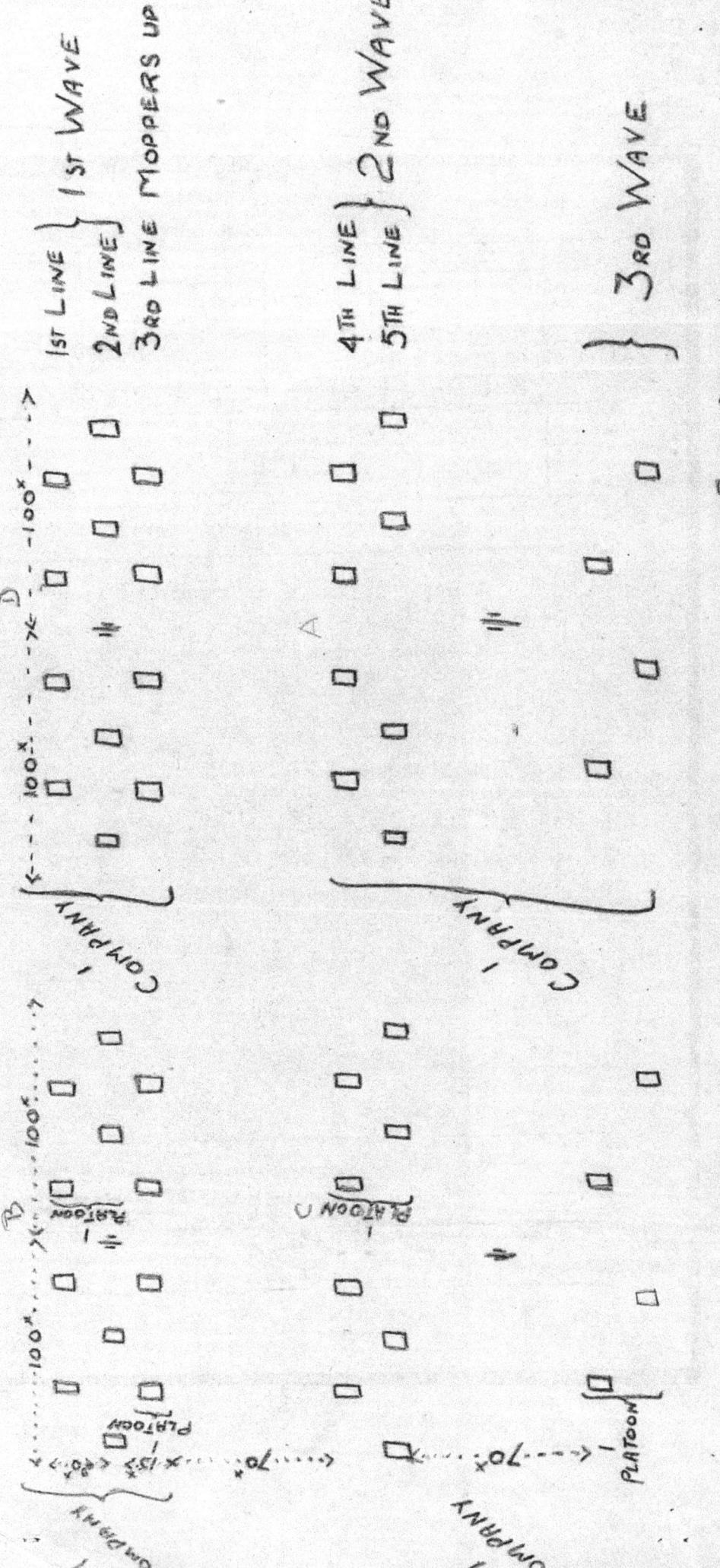

SECRET.   Copy No. 9

Preliminary Instruction No.5.

1. **Playfair.**
   All messages in Playfair Cipher will begin and end with the letter "K".

2. **BAB Code.**
   BAB Code will not be used. Coys will return their copies to the Orderly Room by 2-0 p.m. 16th inst.

3. **Numbers staying out of action.**
   No 10% party will now be left out. The only Other ranks to remain out will be :- C.M.S's Neville and Bothwell, Sergts. Lloyd, Cox and Williams, Corpls. Downey and Ward., Signallers as already arranged, Other Ranks on Courses etc., and Battn. Administrative Portion.

4. **P.H.Helmets.**
   P.H.Helmets will not be taken into action but will be stored with surplus Kits.

5. **Medical Arrangements.**
   R.A.Posts are situated at :-
   J.30.b.2.3.   J.10.b.4.2.   K.19.b.4.6.
   Evacuation by hand and Wheeled Stretchers to A.D.S. at J.29.a.5.0., WINDY CORNER, HERMIES.
   A walking wounded post is situated behind SLAG HEAP in J.34.

6. **Water.**
   All water bottles will be filled before leaving Assembly Positions. No water will be brought up before Z plus 1 Night.

7. **Villages.**
   If a village is taken which is occupied by civilians, care will be taken not to allow civilians outside the confines of the village.

8. **Surplus Kit (Other Ranks)**
   On notice being given to pack surplus Kits, each man will be issued with a sandbag. He will take an inventory of his kit, have it signed by an officer and place it inside of sandbag which will then be securely tied and marked with owners Regtl.No., Name, Rank, and Regiment with indelible pencil.

=================

Addendum to P.I's No.3 and No.4.

1. **Prisoners.**
   Prisoners cage is situated at J.29.a.5.1. W.of HERMIES.

2. **Casualties.**
   In the event of Officers and Other Ranks being reported Missing believed Killed, Missing believed Wounded, or Wounded and Missing, Coys. will forward a short precis of the evidence from which it is assumed the officer or men is Missing etc. together with Casualty report.

Field,   Captain and Adjutant,
16-11-17   1st Battalion Royal Irish Fusiliers.

SPECIAL BATTALION ORDER.

Brigadier-General R.J.Kentish wishes to express to all ranks the intense pleasure it gave him, when on his visit to the Battalion last week, to find it in such splendid order. The appearance of all ranks, though in the trenches, the alertness of the Sentries, the state of the Arms and the cleanliness of the trenches were all, in his opinion, a fine example of what can be done when the Officers, Non-Commissioned Officers and Men in a Battalion are all inbued with one aim and one object, viz., to keep and maintain for ever the honour and reputation of the Regiment. He feels, that as long as this spirit permeates the Battalion it can never look back, and even though it may be presumtion on his part to say so, he cannot refrain from congratulating from the bottom of his heart all those splendid Officers, Non-Commissioned Officers and Private Soldiers of the 87th whom he had the pleasure of meeting, and some of whom have fought for 40 months without a break, on their magnificent spirit and determination to preserve the honour of the King - their Colonel-in-Chief - of their Country and of their Regiment to the end.

-------oOo-------

S E C R E T.   Copy No.

Preliminary Instruction No. 3.

1. **Ruses.**

    It must be impressed on all Officers and Other Ranks that the command "Retire" does not exist and is frequently used by the enemy in the hope of deceiving.
    Anyone giving this command must be treated as an enemy.

2. **Casualties.**

    (a) Wounded Men must not be allowed to discard their equipment or arms unless their wounds are so severe as to render the men incapable of carrying them.
    Slightly wounded men who disobey this order will be detained and sent back.
    (b) Slightly Wounded Officers and Men will continue to take part in Operations until ordered to the rear by a superior officer. The presence of a wounded Officer, N.C.O., or Men in the ranks who, though being wounded has the grit to continue fighting, is most inspiring to his comrades.

3. **Prisoners.**

    Escort to Prisoners will not exceed 10% of number of prisoners in batch. Prisoners should, if possible, be kept until a large number has been collected.

4. **Water.**

    (a) Great care must be taken in the use of water behind the German Lines. All wells, Pumps, etc must be inspected by a M.O. before being used.
    (b) All ranks must be warned to husband the water in their waterbottles during the attack as water may not be available for over 36 hours.

5. **Documents.**

    SS 135 para. XXXIII reads :-
    "All ranks taking part in assault are forbidden to carry any
    "letters, papers, orders or sketches, which in the event of their
    "capture would be likely to give any information to the enemy".

Field,
13-11-17

Captain and Adjutant,
1st Battalion Royal Irish Fusiliers.

War Diary Appendix "H"

MALPLAQUET HOUSE,
MARLBOROUGH LINES,
ALDERSHOT.

October 30. 1917.

Dear Webber,

If you approve will you kindly have the special order inserted in Battalion Orders, and issue the other letter to each of the Companies when they are in Billets.

I do very heartily congratulate you on the splendid state of the Regiment, and I cannot tell you how delighted I was to see them all again, and looking so splendid and well.

I was very greatly impressed by the manner in which the Sentries in the Line and in the forward Saps received me; and also with the knowledge of the Officers and N.C.O's.

The appearance of the Officers was really excellent, and in itself the secret of the good state of the whole Battalion. I have said all I wish to say in my letter and order to the Companies. I can only repeat to you again that it is a great privilege and pleasure to be given the opportunity of visiting the old Regiment, and of finding them after 40 months of War more efficient than ever.

I give you my best congratulations on your promotion to Command a Brigade, and I wish you the best of luck in your new Command.

I am going to raise the necessary subscription to provide for turkeys for the Battalion this Christmas as I did last year, and will send you a line later.

Yours ever,

N. J. Nicholl

Brig-General Incledon Webber, D.S.O.,

Operation Orders
by
Lieut.Colonel, M. J. F U R N E L L.,
Commanding 1st Battalion Royal Irish Fusiliers.,

In the Field, 28-11-17.

-:-

1. **MOVE.**

The Battalion less transport will entrain at YTRES tomorrow at 9-0 a.m. for FOSSEUX Area. Length of journey 4½ hours.

The Battalion will parade on road outside camp at 7-0 a.m. facing BUS, head of column resting at the BUS end of the Camp.

Order of March :- Hd.Qrs., A, B, C, D.Coys.

Dress :- F.S.M.O. Leather Jerkins will be folded below supporting straps at top of the pack.

Breakfasts will be served at 5-30 a.m.

Route :- BUS - LECHELLE - YTRES.

Rations for the 30th inst will be issued at YTRES. Officers should carry Haversack Rations.

Transport :- All articles for transport will be ready for loading by 6-0 a.m. Officers Valices, Orderly Room Kit, and 1 Mess Box per Coy. and Bn.Hd.Qrs. will be stacked ready for loading on Lorry, close to the road at the BUS end of the Camp, by 6-30 a.m.

1 Blanket per man will be issued tomorrow morning and will be carried by N.C.O's and Men.

Captain and Adjutant,
1st Battalion Royal Irish Fusiliers.

War Diary

SECRET

APPENDIX 5.

107th Infantry Brigade Instructions for the Offensive.

COMMUNICATIONS IN THE ATTACK.

1. The 8/9th R.I.Rifles, and 1st R.I.Fus, will each collect ½mile of cable from the same place.

    The greatest economy must be exercised in the use of cable as otherwise it is feared that the supply will fail in the later operations.
    All empty drums should be returned through Brigade to the HERMIES DUMP.

2. Battalion Signal Stations will be marked by day by a flag Signalling Flag, (White blue band) and at light by a light screened by transparent blue paper paper.

    From Zero onwards the restrictions on the use of the Telephone will be removed but will be put into force again in the event of operations assuming a stationary character.

    Fullerphones will be left behind with the 33% of Signallers in reserve.

VISUAL SIGNALLING. A Divisional Visual Station will be established at approximately K.I.a.Y.U. on the afternoon of "Z" day. This station will work to all Stations it can see.

Efforts will be made to establish a Visual Station as near Brigade Headquarters as possible. Where possible Battalion Stations will work to this Station.

The red screen will always be used for Lucas Lamps at night.

It should be impressed on all Signallers, that they will accept all messages irrespective of who offers them.

Signalling shutters will be used by day wherever possible in order to save Lucas Lamps.

Instructions as to Visual procedure have been sent to all Signalling Officers.

PIGEONS. One pair of pigeons per day /will be allotted to each of the four Battalions. These will be collected from Brigade Headquarters SLAG HEAP after 8p.m on "Z" day.

Pigeons will be supplied in "Assault" baskets with message pads clips and pencil. They must be released before 3-30 p.m. on Zero plus 1 day.

A supply will probably be available at Brigade Headquarters each day. It is of great importance that all empty baskets should be returned at once to Brigade Headquarters.

CODE CALLS. The call of the Divisional Visual Station will be "A.V"
The power Buzzers will use the Station call to which they are attached.

MAINTAINANCE. The responsibility for lateral communication will in all cases be from left to right.

18/11/17.

S E C R E T .   Copy No.
                        Preliminary Instructions NO 9.

1. The Battalion will move to the Assembly positions P.4.a.8.8. starting
from this Camp at Zero hour plus 25 mins.

   The Battalion, less details will parade at Zero plus 15 minutes on the
Football Ground in Column of Company's. facing South.

   1 marker per Coy. and 1 from H.Qrs. will report to the R.S.M. 5 mins.
before hour of parade.

   Order of parade march- H.Qrs., D.B.A.C. Coy's. 100 yds. between Coy's.

   Battn. pass a starting point Road Junction P.20.b.5.2. at Zero plus
45 minutes.

   Route- RUYAULCOURT- P.4.c. and a.

   Regt. Transport, less L.Gun Limbers, will march with the Brigade Trans.
   Lewis Gun Limbers will go with Coy's.
   Lewis Gun Limbers at the Assembly Positions will remain ready in case
it is permitted to use them for carrying forward for some distance
Lewis Guns and Magazines.

   Breakfasts will be at Zero minus plus 1 hour.

   Soup will be ready at Assembly Positions if the Battn. do not move
forwards at Zero plus 2½ to 3 hours, (Limbers if Possible)

   2 O.R's "C" Coy. for Brigade Intelligence, will report at Bde. H.Qrs.
at J.34.c.8.5. at Zero plus 2 hours to 2/Lt. Tooley, M.C.

   Details. All details will parade under Major G.W.P. Hornidge, M.C. at
Zero plus 45 mins. and march to details Camp at near VELU.
Senior Mess. W.O. or N.C.O., of details of each Coy. etc. will be in
possession of a Nominal Roll of their party, and hand it to Major.
Hornidge on parade.

   Officers Valise Wagon will accompany Battn. details, dump Officers Mess
details kits at their camp and then join Regt. Transport at the SLAG
HEAP.
   Officers Valises will be stacked in 2 distinct piles i.e . 1 for Offs.
details and the other for all other Officer of the Battn. outside the
Orderly Room at 4-45 p.m.
   2/LT. G.W.R. Templer will superintend and have details kits and those
got on last on the G.S. Waggon.

Field   Capt. & Adjt.
10/11/17   1st Battalion Royal Irish Fusiliers.

S E C R E T .   Copy No.

Preliminary Instruction No.7.

1. Stores.
The following stores will be issued at assembly positions P.6.a.
West of Slag Heap.
(All numbers approximate).

S.A.A.	16,000 rnds.	
No.5 Mills	480 per Coy.	Rifle Grenadiers will carry 2 Bombs 2 per bomber and 2 bombs per O.R.
No.23 Rifle Grenades.	25 per Coy.	2 per Rifle Grenadier.
No.24 " "	27 " "	2 per " "
SDB or P.Bomb	14 for B & D Coys.For Moppers up.	
	8 " A & C " For Bombing Section.	
1" Very Lights	25 per Coy.	
	27 Bn.Hd.Qrs.	
Aeroplane flares-White.	70 packets per Coy.	
	30 Bn.Hd.Qrs.	
S.O.S.Rifle Grenades.	5 Tubes per Coy.	
	5 Bn.HH.Qrs.	
Sand bags.	620 per Coy.	2 per man.
	80 Bn.Hd.Qrs.	

Stores carried by Bn.Hd.Qrs.are a small reserve for Coys. in case of emergency. Stores will be laid out by Coys.

2. Very Pistols.
Coys will carry 8 per Coy. Bn.Hd.Qrs will carry 16, 2 as reserve for each Coy.

3. Transport.
Transport Lines on Z Day will be at Assembly Positions P.6.a.
Tents and Shelters for Transport Personnel will be available on Z Day at P.6.a.O.S.

4. Details.
Officers and Other Ranks left out of action will be accomodated in huts at I.29.d.7.8. and will proceed there on Z Day. Details can keep one Blanket per man which they will have to carry.
Brigade N.C.O's Class will rejoin the Battn. on 19th inst. and will move with Details on Zero Day.

5. Contact Aeroplanes.
Aeroplane flares will be lit by the most advanced line of troops only and only when called for by contact aeroplane by the firing of Very Light or Klaxton Horn. Flares should be lit in groups of three every 60 to 70 yards. Flares are not all to be expended at once.

6. "Lengthen Range" Signal.
Red flares will be issued at the Assembly positions. Signal for the Artillery to "Lift Barrage" or "Start rolling barrage forward" will be 3 Very Lights, WHITE,RED,WHITE fired in quick succession.

7. Discipline.
From Zero everyone is ready for action at any moment. No one will be allowed to fall out after leaving Assembly Position and no one must go souvenir hunting, even if the Battn. is halted.

8. Brigade Intelligence.
Every Coy will detail 2 Corpls & Men, equipped as runners, to report to Lieut.XXXXX,I.O. 10th R.Ir.Rifles at Brigade Hd.Qrs. on Zero morning with rations enough for Zero and Zero plus 1 day. They will be working with Brigade Intelligence Section. Time of reporting will be notified later.

9. Surplus Kits. All men's surplus Kits to be ready by Sept. 18th.

10. Synchronisation of Watches. The Signalling Officer will proceed to Bde.Hd. Qrs at 10-30 a.m. daily starting 18th inst. will get time and bring it to Bn.Hd.Qrs.

                                        Captain and Adjutant,
                                        1st Battalion Royal Irish Fusiliers.

S E C R E T.   Copy No.

Preliminary Instruction No.6.

1. **Continuation of Para 4 Preliminary Instructions No.1.**

   (a) As soon as the FLESQUIERES and the HINDENBURG System (known as the BROWN LINE) have been captured the 51st Division will capture CANTAING and FONTAINE-NOTRE DAME, and put out outposts to the North and East.

   (b) The 62nd Division will clear the HINDENBURG System Support System up to the place where it crosses the ridge in E.29. An attack will also be made on GRAINCOURT and the Bridge on the BAPAUME-CAMBRAI Road. Immediately GRAINCOURT has been captured, an Advanced Guard of all arms will move on ANNEUX, capture that, gain possession of the High ground West of BOURLON WOOD and assist the 1st Cavalry Division in the capture of the village if they are not already in possession of it. They will then take it over from the cavalry - 2 Squadrons of King Edward's Horse will be attached to the 62nd Division for the purpose - Both the 51st and 62nd Divisions will push out reconnaissances as soon as they can after the capture of the BROWN LINE.

   (c) The 36th Division will effect a junction with the 109th Brigade wherever the attack finally reaches. The dividing line between the 109th Brigade and the 36th Division will be the grid line between squares K.7 & 8 or its continuation Northwards.

2. Paras. 7 and 8 of Preliminary Instruction No. 1 are cancelled and the following substituted :-

   The 107th and 108th Infantry Brigades will assemble in J.34.c. and P.4.a probably at Zero plus 3 hours. From this position they will be able to move along the canal, or by the HERMIES-GRAINCOURT Road as the situation permits, to the German System West of FLESQUIERES.

3. The 36th Division will carry out very active patrolling to get early information if the enemy retire from their front. They will be prepared to advance at once in case of their doing so.

4. After the capture of the BROWN LINE, 4 Brigades of Field Artillery and 1 Horse Battery of 60 Pounders, and 1 of 6" Howitzers will be allotted to this Division.

5. The road which will be utilised in the first place for the forward movement of the 36th Division is the HERMIES-GRAINCOURT Road. C.R.E. will arrange to have all material for a bridge to carry normal traffic (G.S.Wagons and Field Guns) loaded on wagons and ready to move up at once to bridge the canal at E.16-a.4.5. A Bridge for Infantry and Pack animals will also be prepared for erection just South of the SLAG HEAP, K.30 Central, or any place which proves more suitable as the situation develops.

Field,
19-11-17

(sd) W. Scott
Captain and Adjutant,
1st Battalion Royal Irish Fusiliers.

- TO ALL RANKS OF THE 87th -

I cannot tell you how delighted I was to see you all last week, and more especially delighted to find the Battalion in such splendid form. Personally, I do not think the Battalion has ever been in such good order during this War as it is to-day, and considering the fact that you have been fighting hard for over three years the state of things prevailing is one that reflects the very greatest credit on all concerned. Three things impressed me more than anything else, and I can only tell you that with all the experience of men and things I have been fortunate enough to gain, both before and in this War, that as long as you keep all three uppermost in your minds the Battalion will ever retain its splendid reputation. Those important matters are:-

(a) The soldierly appearance of all ranks, alertness of Officers and N.C.O's, and Men, and consequently

(b) The excellent order I found things in, in the trenches, both by night and by day, and

(c) The cleanliness of the Arms.

With regard to (a), the Officers, though in the trenches, were soldierly, clean and well-turned out, and the same may be said of the Non-Commissioned Officers and Men, and the turn out and appearance of the group of Non-Commissioned Officers, and of the Drummers I saw in the Village behind the Line reminded me of the 87th in the old days before the War.

With regard to (b), I found Officers and Non-Commissioned Officers who knew their work, and Men as alert on Sentry as any I have ever come across, and the manner in which I was received when turning a traverse at night, viz., with the bayonet at my throat, and in the day by the Sentry manning his Post in a clean and soldierly manner told me all the time of the splendid state of the Battalion.

And with regard to (c), at 'Stand-to' on Tuesday, I saw in front of me, after three years and four months of War, the same splendid system of cleaning the rifles and ammunition as obtained when I was Commanding "A" Company, and consequently when later in the morning I again went round the line I found the rifles in perfect order.

You have, after over three years' of fighting alongside your old friends in the Fourth Division, now left them to join your present Division. This in itself would have been sufficient to temporarily depress you, and possibly to affect your efficiency, but nothing of the kind has occurred, and your state to-day shows that you are as determined as ever to allow nothing to stand between you, and your determination to keep the Battalion in the highest state of efficiency.

In any case, if you have lost friends - very old friends - in one Division, you have found and quickly made new friends with your new Division, and especially so is this the case with our 9th Battalion, whose Officers and Men I met. Everyone of them expressed their joy at having you with them for, as their Commanding Officer said to me, "It would be an incentive to us to emulate them, and we are going to try and beat them at everything!!"

P.T.O.

- continued -

I finish this letter to you by assuring you that no stone will be left unturned in our efforts to keep our own Officers always at the head of the 87th, and all other Battalions of the Regiment, and you will, I am sure, be delighted to know that, at the time of writing, an Officer of the Royal Irish Fusiliers is Commanding every one of our Battalions. I tell you this that you may know that we Senior Officers of the Regiment are always thinking of you and guarding your interests even if we may not be with you.

Good Luck to you all, and never forget that "His Majesty the King is our Colonel-in-Chief".

N.R. Hea1tThrig. General

Operation Order No 87 "A"2

Lt Col A B Beckwith-Smith DSO
Comdg 1st Batt. Regt. Irish Fusiliers
1.8.17

Move 1. Batt. will entrain at Arras at
4.54 pm for HOU POUTRE
Length of journey about 6 hours.

Batt. will parade at 2.20pm on ground
opposite rear Bn HQrs (water bottles filled)
Regt. Master for day to report to RSM
at Batt HQrs at 2.10 pm
Order of march = HQ, B D A
Route 1:- BLANGY Lock — BLANGY —
C 23 d 6.8 — Arras station.
Guide will be met at C 28 b 4.2
at 3.30pm who will conduct batt. to
Assembly Place where tea will be
served at 4 pm

Party for 2 "C" Coy will parade at 12 noon
Entraining & proceed to Arras station & report
Transport to DAAQMG at RTO office
C 28 c 2.4 at 1.50 pm
Dinners for this party will be
taken in Arras station at 1 pm

CONFIDENTIAL

- WAR DIARY -

OF

1st. BATTALION ROYAL IRISH FUSILIERS

PERIOD

1 - 12 - 17. TO 31 - 12 - 17.

M.J. Furnell Lieut. Colonel,
Commanding 1st Battalion Royal Irish Fusiliers.

Field.
1-1-18.

Army Form C. 2118.

WAR DIARY
or
INTELLIGENCE SUMMARY.
(Erase heading not required.)

Instructions regarding War Diaries and Intelligence Summaries are contained in F. S. Regs. Part II. and the Staff Manual respectively. Title pages will be prepared in manuscript.

Place	Date	Hour	Summary of Events and Information	Remarks and references to Appendices
In the Field.	13-12-17.		inthe Front Line about ¾ mile S. of MARCOING, relief complete by 10-30 p.m. Weather Fine. Quiet.	n/f.
	14-12-17.		Holding Front Line "Outpost Line" Slight Enemy shelling, no casualties.	n/f.
	15-12-17.		Still holding Outposts, Line. Situation normal.	n/f.
	16-12-17.		Relieved by 1/4th K.S.L.I., and proceeded to Billets in METZ. Relief complete by 12 M.M.	n/f.
	17-12-17.		Moved to ETRICOURT by route march at 1-44 p.m. Details rejoined Battn., from SOREL-LE-GRAND, Transport also rejoined.	n/f.
	18-12-17.		Moved to IVERGNY. Entrained at ETRICOURT at 11 a.m. and detrained at MONDICOURT at 3-30 p.m. Marched to IVERGNY, in Billets by 7 p.m. Transport travelling by march route, reached IVERGNY 20th inst.	n/f.
	19-12-17.		Billets IVERGNY. Battn. employed clearing roads of snow etc., Arrivals:- Lieut. B.L. Beckingsale 2/Lt. A.J. Rogers, 2/Lt. JTJ. Michie, 2/Lt. J. Bridges.	n/f.
	20-12-17.		Moved from IVERGNY to SUS ST LEGER. Battn. employed clearing roads of snow by route march, distance 3 Kilometres. Move complete by 3 p.m. Arrivals:- 2/Lt R.L. Connar,	n/f.
	21-12-17.		Billets SUS ET LEGER. Battn. employed clearing roads of snow . Drill parades, Kit inspection. Weather very cold.	n/f.
	22-12-17.		As for the 21st.	n/f.
	23-12-17.		As for the 21-12-17.	n/f.
	24-12-17.		As for the 21st.	n/f.
	25-12-17.		Christmas was celebrated. Companies had dinners in Estaminets, the Turkeys did not turn up. Officers and Sgts. had dinners in the evening. Snow in the evening.	n/f.
	26-12-17.		Companies parade. Still very cold.	n/f.
	27-12-17.		Battn. parades at 4-30 a.m. and marched 8 miles to MONDICOURT to entrain for CORBIE at 9 a.m.	n/f.

Army Form C. 2118.

WAR DIARY
or
INTELLIGENCE SUMMARY.
(Erase heading not required.)

Instructions regarding War Diaries and Intelligence Summaries are contained in F. S. Regs., Part II. and the Staff Manual respectively. Title pages will be prepared in manuscript.

Place	Date	Hour	Summary of Events and Information	Remarks and references to Appendices
In the field.	1-12-17.		Battalion marched on night of Nov 30-Dec1st, from BERNAVILLE to COURCELLES LE COMTE en route for the Trenches, the Division having been recalled to the Line. Battn. moved from COURCELLES LE COMTE to BEAULENCOURT by route march. 2/Lt. J. McMorran proceeded 29th Nov. to join Indian Army Reserve of Officers onprobation.	Appx.
	2-12-17.		Battn. moved from BEAULENCOURT to LECHELLE Area by route march. 2/Lt. C.P. Domegan left for R.F.C.	Appx.
	3-12-17.		Battn. moved to Trenches E. of TRESCAULT. Details to MANANCOURT, Transport to near FINS.	Appx.
	4-12-17.		Battn moved from LECHELLE and went into Division Reserve Trenches about ¾ mile E. of TRESCAULT. Weather very cold. Details to MANANCOURT, Regt. Transport to SOREL-LE-GRAND.	Appx.
	5-12-17.		Very cold, Battn. awaiting orders, Still in Reserve Trenches. Lieut. E.J. Parkhill to Hospital.	Appx.
	6-12-17.		Very cold but dry. Still in Reserve Trenches.	Appx.
	7-12-17.		Weather milder. Working party of 4 Officers and 200 O.R's detailed for Wiring Front Line, at 5 p.m.	Appx.
	8-12-17.		Relieved the 9th R.Innis, Fus. in Brigade Reserve Trenches about 1 mile S.E. of RIBECOURT. Relief complete by 10-30 p.m. Weather fine and mild. Details moved from MANANCOURT to SOREL-LE-GRAND.	Appx.
	9-12-17.		Still in Brigade Reserve line. Quiet. Slight rain.	Appx.
	10-12-17.		Working parties for Front Line 170 strong. QUIET. Weather mild.	Appx.
	11e12-17.		Fine. Whole Battn. on working parties. Major G.M.P. Hornidge,M.C. taked over temporary Command of the 10th R.I.Rif.	Appx.
	12-12-17.		Quiet. Weather fine. Whole Battn. on working parties.	Appx.
	13-12-17.		Battn . very weak numerically formed into 2 Coy's. 2 Coy's./10th R.I.Rif. attached to Battn. and came under Command of Lieut. Col. M.J. Furnell. Relieved the 11/13th R.I.Rif. 108th b108th Bde.	Appx.

A5834 Wt. W4973 M687 750,000 8/16 D.D.&L.Ltd Forms/C.2118/13.

Army Form C. 2118.

WAR DIARY
or
INTELLIGENCE SUMMARY.
(Erase heading not required.)

Instructions regarding War Diaries and Intelligence Summaries are contained in F. S. Regs., Part II. and the Staff Manual respectively. Title pages will be prepared in manuscript.

Place	Date	Hour	Summary of Events and Information	Remarks and references to Appendices
In the Field.	27-12-17.		Battn arrived at CORBIE at 1 p.m and Billeted in FOUILLOY.	appx.
	28-12-17.		Lewis Gun special training and Company training.	appx.
	29-12-17.		Same as 28th.	appx.
	30-12-17		Church parades.	appx.
	31-12-17.		Training continued.	appx.

Appendix "A" War Diary.
1st Battalion The Royal Irish Fusiliers.

Date.	O.R's.	Officers.	Officers name.	Remarks.
Jan 1.	3			
2.	3			
3.	1			
4.	-			
5.	-			
6.	1			
7.	3			
8.	1			
9.	1			
10.	-			
11.	16			
12.	8			
13.	15			
14.	-			
15.	-			
16.	-			
17.	-			
18.	2			
19.	4			
20.	2	1	Lieut J.I.Smith.	
21.	19	1	A/Capt Hartley.	
22.	9			
23.	-			
24.	-			
25.	10			
26.	-			
27.	29			
28.	32	2	(2/Lieut Donagh	
29.	8		(" McCartney.	
30.	-			
31.	-			
Total.	140.	4.	Grand Total. 144.	

LIEUTENANT COLONEL.
Commanding..
1st Battalion The Royal Irish Fusiliers...

www.ingramcontent.com/pod-product-compliance
Lightning Source LLC
Chambersburg PA
CBHW081557160426
43191CB00011B/1956